Oxford Secondary English

Book 2

John Seely

and
Frank Ash
Frank Green
Chris Woodhead

Oxford
University
Press

Oxford University Press, Walton Street, Oxford OX2 6DP

Oxford New York Toronto
Delhi Bombay Calcutta Madras Karachi
Petaling Jaya Singapore Hong Kong Tokyo
Nairobi Dar es Salaam Cape Town
Melbourne Auckland

and associated companies in
Beirut Berlin Ibadan Nicosia

Oxford is a trade mark of Oxford University Press

© Oxford University Press 19

First published 1982
Reprinted 1982, 1983 (twice), 1984, 1985, 1986

ISBN 0 19 831135 4

John Seely is the author of *Dramakit*
and *Playkits* (OUP)

Printed in Great Britain by
Scotprint, Musselburgh

There is a pupil's book and a teacher's book for each
year of *Oxford Secondary English*. The teacher's
book is an integral part of the course and contains
reproducible assignments on the material in the
pupil's book. Notes and advice for the teacher are
also included.

Contents

Section A: Themes and Specials

Section B: Skills

at kind of courage
he people in these
tographs need?

COURAGE

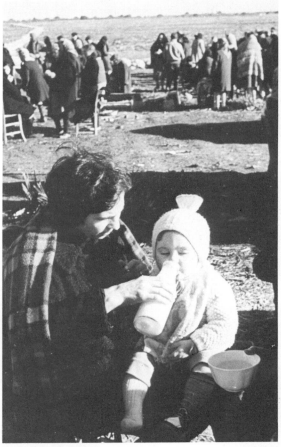

Keep hold of yourself

While exploring an empty house, Lennie has been bitten in the leg by a rattlesnake. He tries to make his way home, but quickly becomes weak with pain.

Lennie took a deep breath and tried to push himself into a sitting position. He fell back on his elbow. He tried again. He couldn't make it. He lay back on the porch.

The silence around him was awful now. It wasn't only the silence that bothered Lennie. It was the terrible feeling that everything had stopped moving. The sun wasn't dropping in the sky. It was still hanging in the sky in exactly the same place. The wind wasn't blowing. The clouds weren't moving. The trees were as still as plastic arrangements.

He closed his eyes. He had lost track of time. He didn't know how long he had been lying here. It seemed like days. Years. Centuries.

Now, lying on the porch, dying, he sent out a mental signal to the world. 'Come! Come! Come!' Silently he willed the invisible people with all his might. 'Anyone within range of my mind, come! Help me! Help!'

His leg jerked again and he cried out. He put his fists up to his eyes.

'You have to keep hold of yourself,' his mom had told him once. It was just after her boyfriend Sam had died. Lennie had been sad too. Sam was his favourite of his mother's boyfriends. Sam had owned a diner and was so big and strong he flattened hamburgers like he was swatting flies. He was always saying, 'Hit me, kid, go ahead and hit me as hard as you can'.

Lennie would hit and hit until his arms got tired, but it was like trying to hurt a mattress. Lennie liked it when he couldn't hurt Sam. It was nice to know that there was one person in the world who could not be hurt no matter what you did.

And then Sam had died. He died right at the diner while he was shovelling snow off the parking-lot. His heart, it turned out, was not as strong as his body.

Lennie had sat in the last booth with his mom while she warmed her hands round a cup of coffee.

'You always have to keep hold of yourself,' she said.

Lennie had a young-looking mother. People were always mistaking her for his sister. Now for the first time she looked old enough really to be his mother.

She wrapped her arms round herself. 'Never let go, Lennie.'

'I try not to.'

'No matter what happens.'

'Will we have to leave the diner?'

She nodded.

'But where will we go?'

'I don't know, but if we just keep hold of ourselves we'll be all right.'

'I'll try to.'

Now, as if to keep his word, Lennie hugged himself. One arm was on each shoulder, but his fingers were like icy claws. There was no comfort. He wished for dream arms that would grow long on command and wrap him like soft fleshy hoses.

Holding himself tighter, he sent out the message again. Somebody, anybody, come.

Betsy Byars, *The TV Kid*

Questions to think and talk about	1 What was Lennie frightened of?
	2 Why did he suddenly remember Sam?
	3 How did he feel about Sam?
	4 What did his mother's advice mean?
	5 Was Lennie being brave?

Writing Not all frightening experiences are as dramatic as this. Sometimes they can be quite everyday things, like:

> going to the dentist
> being sent to the Head
> riding a bike without brakes

1 Choose a frightening experience from everyday life.

2 Describe the thoughts that go through your head as you face up to it.

3 Now do a second piece of writing. A friend asks you 'What was it like?' Write the conversation that follows.

Children against the jungle

It was a noisy take-off. As the single-engined Cessna aircraft rose above the Amazonian jungle in Peru, its nine child passengers were laughing and looking forward to their long Christmas holiday at home.

Oscar Zehnder, the young pilot, knew most of the children. He worked for the small airline that served settlements in isolated parts of Peru. With him was his seventeen-year-old sister Grace. At 13.40 hours, twenty-five minutes after take-off and at a height of 7,500 feet, Oscar realized that the plane was in trouble. The engine began to miss and then cut out. The plane went into a dive. There was no radio on board so he could not send out a distress call. He told the children to hold on for a crash landing.

The plane broke up as it hit the trees, although Oscar had reduced speed as much as possible before impact. When Grace stumbled from the wreck, she saw Antonio's body on the ground. Six-year-old Juan was bleeding from his nose and mouth and he died as she held him. With her bloodstained fingers she made the sign of the cross on the small boy's forehead.

Oscar was unconscious. The other children seemed only slightly injured, except for Kathy, whose legs were both broken. Grace realized that she must take charge. The smell of petrol spread around them. 'Get out! Get out!' she shouted. Together they pulled Oscar from his cabin. He regained consciousness three hours later.

They were not afraid of the jungle itself. They knew well its sounds and sights. But they were unable to move yet; they were surrounded by thick vegetation, and it began to thunder and rain long into the night. They got no sleep, and their two dead companions were constantly in their minds.

In the morning Oscar had recovered. He found a little food in the wreckage, and pulled out two machetes and a revolver. They would set off on a long journey to the nearest settlement. They left the bodies of Antonio and Juan by the wreckage. Grace and Oscar took turns in carrying Kathy.

In the jungle 100 metres can be a long way. In the sticky heat they soon became thirsty. They found a waterhole and drank though the water was bitter. They ate some berries. Already they were very tired. Kathy kept fainting from pain. Then, to their horror they found that they had gone in a circle and were back to where they started.

Problem 1 Read the passage.
2 Look at the pictures.
3 Decide what you would do next, if you were Grace or Oscar.
4 Write it down.
5 *Do NOT read anything else on this page until you are told to.*

Wrong order The rest of the story is told below but it is in the wrong order. Sort out what the correct order should be and write down the numbers of the sections in that order.

1 Oscar killed several snakes with a machete.
   On the seventh day the rain was so heavy they could hardly see.

2 When Oscar laid her down, she, too, was dead.
   The group were welcomed by the Indian peasant farmers, who gave them shelter and brought them soup and sweet potatoes.

3 The second night was cold. It poured with rain, and gave them water to drink. They still had hope. Next morning they heard aircraft overhead but knew they could not be seen through the ceiling of trees. They had no matches to light a fire for smoke.

4 'We've done it! We've done it!' Oscar shouted. But Kathy did not hear the shouts of joy and relief.

5 By the third night Oscar was very worried. Several times they had travelled in circles. Several of the children were being sick. Kathy was crying softly.

6 They struggled on. Two hours later they suddenly cut their way into a clearing where a few huts were standing.

7 The following days were much the same. They made slow progress. Small cuts were now swollen with infection, and made worse by mosquitoes and maggots that seemed to be everywhere.

Using your own ideas

These are extracts from different pieces of writing about courage and fear.

Courage

What makes people unsatisfied
is that they accept lies.

If people had courage, and refused lies
and found out what they really felt and really meant
and acted on it . . . .

How would you continue this poem?

In the wood

'It's a noise. There's something through there.'
'What?'
'I don't know, do I?'
'It can't be any person, that isn't a person's noise.'
'No.'
'It's stopped now.'
'Perhaps it's gone away, then.'
The twigs cracked again, and then they heard soft, thudding steps in the leaf-mould out beyond the bushes.
'Go and look.'
'It might be . . .'
'What?'
'I don't know.'
'Go and look.'
Silence.
'You're scared.'
'So are you, then.'
'Don't be stupid.'
'Why daren't you go out?'
'I said it first, you've got to go. *Go on* . . .'

Who are they?
Why are they there?
What happens next?

Martin Luther King

In Montgomery, Alabama, in the 1950s there were separate sections for white and black people on buses.

On 1st December, a Negro seamstress named Rosa Parks, tired from working all day and shopping, refused to give up her seat on the bus to a white passenger. She later said that she had not planned to do what she did: 'I was just plain tired, and my feet hurt.' The bus driver called a policeman, who arrested Mrs. Parks. She was taken to the courthouse. There she was allowed to phone a man named E. D. Nixon, who was to come down and sign bail for her. E. D. Nixon, a Civil Rights activist† in Montgomery, had seen his people pushed around for years. He was tired of it, he had had enough.

Suddenly it seemed as if all Negroes in Montgomery felt that way too. A one-day boycott of the buses was planned to protest at the treatment of Negroes on the buses in Montgomery and throughout the whole state of Alabama. E. D. Nixon rang Dr. King and said, 'We have taken this type of thing too long. I feel the time has come to boycott★ the buses. It's the only way to make the white folks see that we will not take this sort of thing any longer.'

On the day of the boycott, the Kings were up at dawn. Dr. King was in the kitchen when the first bus came along the road. 'Martin! Martin! Come quickly!' called his wife. He ran to look: the bus was completely empty. So was the bus after that, and the one after that. Dr. King jumped into his car and drove around the city, looking at empty bus after empty bus. He felt that a miracle had happened. Negroes were walking, riding mules, driving wagons – anything to stay off the buses.

That same Monday morning Rosa Parks was convicted and fined ten dollars. Dr. King and the other Negro leaders held a meeting in the afternoon. They decided to extend the boycott until the bus company met certain minimal demands. They founded the Montgomery Improvement Association (M.I.A.) and Dr. King was asked to be the President.

The position of President was a dangerous one. It meant being singled out as the key leader of the boycott and the target for white people's anger. Dr. King accepted readily and courageously. At the meeting it was suggested that the Association should be kept secret. If no names were mentioned it would not be too dangerous for the

† activist: someone who takes an active part in supporting a cause.
★ boycott: a refusal to use them; for one day no Negro would travel by bus.

leaders. E. D. Nixon did not like that idea: 'We're acting like little boys,' he said. 'Somebody's name will be known, and if we're afraid we might just as well fold up right now. The white folks are going to find out anyway. We'd better decide now if we are going to be fearless men or scared little boys.'

Dr. King, as President of the Montgomery Improvement Association, was asked to make the main speech at the mass meeting that night. He was nervous about the responsibility. He had to make a speech militant enough to inspire his people to action, and yet it was not in him to arouse hate or resentment.

He arrived at the meeting that night to find that five thousand people had gathered. After the cheers which greeted his arrival had died down, he spoke: '. . . there comes a time,' he said, 'when people get tired. We are here this evening to say to those who have mistreated us so long, that we are tired. Tired of being segregated and humiliated, tired of being kicked about by the brutal feet of oppression. We have no alternative but to protest . . . we have been amazingly patient. But we come here tonight to be saved from the patience that makes us patient with anything less than freedom and justice.'

He talked about the comparisons the newspapers were making between the Montgomery Improvement Association and the Ku

Klux Klan, 'They are protesting for the perpetuation of injustice. We're protesting for the birth of justice . . . their methods lead to violence and lawlessness, but in our protest there will be no cross burnings, no white person will be taken from his home by a hooded Negro mob and brutally murdered . . . we will be guided by the highest principles of law and order . . . If you will protest courageously and yet with dignity and Christian love, future historians will say, "There lived a great people – a black people – who injected new meaning and dignity into the veins of civilization." This is our challenge and our overwhelming responsibility.'

When he had finished speaking, the crowd rose cheering. In that speech, Dr. King had set the tempo and tenor of the movement he was to lead.

One night shortly after that, just after Dr. King had gone to bed, the telephone rang. 'Listen, nigger, we've taken all we want from you; before next week you'll be sorry you ever came to Montgomery.'

Three evenings later the bombing occurred. Mrs. King was chatting with a friend in the living room when there was a thud on the front porch – she later said it sounded like a brick. But the 'brick' went off, shattering the porch and the front windows and filling the house with smoke. Mrs. King, unhurt but terrified, ran to where the baby was asleep at the back of the house. Luckily, Yolanda, too, had come to no harm.

By the time Dr. King, who had been at a meeting, arrived at his home, an angry crowd of Negroes had gathered outside. Police were trying to control the crowd. The situation was extremely dangerous. White reporters who had arrived at the house to cover the story were afraid to leave. The whole thing could have exploded into a disastrous race riot. Dr. King walked out onto his porch. Holding up his hands to silence the crowd he said, 'My wife and baby are all right. I want you to go home and put down your weapons. We cannot solve this problem through retaliatory violence. We must meet violence with non-violence . . . We must meet hate with love. Remember, if I am stopped, this movement will not stop, because God is with this movement.'

The people in the crowd were deeply moved by his words, many were crying. When the Police Commissioner and the Mayor told the crowd that everything possible would be done to find the people who had bombed the Kings' house, people began to drift away. One policeman was heard to say, 'If it hadn't been for the preacher we'd all be dead.'

Patricia Baker, *Martin Luther King*

The shed

Kingshaw is being chased by Hooper in the grounds of the big house, Warings, where they both live.

He had seen the shed before, lots of times, through a gap in the tall hedge that ran round the garden of Warings. There was an allotment, which nobody looked after, and nettles grew, waist-high. At the very bottom, in one corner, was the shed.

Kingshaw ran down the drive, between the rhododendrons, and turned left. A little way along the lane, he stopped and waited. It was very warm. He heard the sound of a tractor up on Dover's Hill. Nothing else. After a moment longer, he began to retrace his steps, keeping close to the bushes, until he came to the broken wire fence at the entrance to the allotment.

There was no sun, only a mass of thick grey cloud, lowering over the countryside, and still, close, thundery air.

The door of the shed was shut, and there was a padlock. But when Kingshaw touched it, his fingers came away brown with powdery rust, and the padlock dropped open.

He wanted to cry with the relief of having escaped from Hooper. He had found a place, he was by himself. He had never dared to come here alone before.

Kingshaw walked forward very cautiously into the shed, smelling his way like an animal.

It was airless and very dark. When the door swung open, a scissor of daylight fell on to the concrete floor, showing clumps of trodden-down straw, and mud. Kingshaw took another step inside, looking anxiously round him. Nothing. Nobody. A pile of old sacks in one corner. He went slowly over to them, and sat down. He was shivering a little.

Seconds later, the door slammed shut. Kingshaw leaped up and ran forward, but as he put his hand out to the door, he heard the click of the padlock. After that, silence.

For a moment or two, he waited. Then he said, 'Hooper?'
Silence.
'Look, I know it's you.'
Silence.
He raised his voice. 'I can get out of here, you needn't think I'm bothered if you've locked the stupid door. I know a way to get out any time I like.'
Silence.

If Hooper had locked him in, then he had been watching out of a window, and then followed him. He was cunning, he could do anything. Yet he had seen and heard nothing, and he had kept on looking back.

He thought, perhaps it isn't Hooper.

The allotment led towards a thick hedge, and then into the fields. It was right away from the village, there never seemed to be anyone about up here. But now there might be. Last year, someone had been strangled to death twenty miles away. Hooper had told him that. Twenty miles wasn't far.

He imagined tramps and murderers, and the cowman at Barr Farm, with bad teeth and hands like raw red meat. Anybody might have been hanging about behind the shed, and locked him in. Later, they might come back.

Sometimes, they were not allowed to see the newspapers, at school, because of things like murder trial reports, but they had them all in the Senior Library, and Lower School boys got sent in there, on messages. If you began to read something, your eyes went on and on, you couldn't stop them until you knew every terrible thing about it, and then you had thoughts and nightmares, you could never return to the time of not-knowing.

He was still standing by the door of the hut. Somebody had used it for animals, once. It smelled faintly of pig muck, and old, dried hen pellets. The walls and roof were made of corrugated metal, bolted together. There was no window, no light at all from anywhere, except for a thin line beneath the door. Kingshaw put out his hands and began to grope his way slowly round until he came to the corner with the sacks. He sat down.

Perhaps they wouldn't wait until night before they came back. Anybody could walk down the allotment and into the shed, and never be seen. They could do anything to him, in here, choke him, or hit him with an axe, or hang him, or stab him, they could get a saw and saw off both his feet and then leave him to bleed. Kingshaw stuffed his fist into his mouth, in terror. Somebody had done that, he'd read it in one of the blood-bath books Ickden had had, last term. Ickden lent them out, at 2d.★ for four days. Kingshaw had read it in the bogs, and wished that he could stop himself and dreaded the nights that came after.

Now, he said to himself, it's Hooper, it's Hooper, there's nobody else it could be. Hooper would be creeping through the grass, back up to the house. Then, he would just wait. Hours and hours, all day, maybe, wait until he decided it was time to let him out.

★ 1p

Kingshaw said aloud, 'I'm not scared of being by myself in the bloody dark.' His voice echoed.

The sacks at the bottom of the pile were damp, and now the damp was coming through. Kingshaw stood up. His jeans felt wet, over his behind. He went back towards the door, and lay down on his side, trying to see out. But the crack was much thinner than he'd thought, now he got down to it, he could see nothing except a faint greyness. He stayed there, pressing his ear to the cold concrete floor of the hut, and straining for the sound of movement, for footsteps. There was nothing.

Then, minutes later, the faint sound of a truck, going down the lane. Kingshaw leaped up, and began to pound and beat upon the door, and then on the corrugated walls, until they crashed and rang in his ears, to scream and yell to be let out, he thought Oh God, God, God, please let somebody come, please let somebody come down the lane, or into the garden, please, Oh God, God, God, God . . .

He gave up. The palms of his hands were hot and throbbing, and the skin had come off one of his knuckles. He sucked at the loose edge, tasting blood. Silence.

Hooper might have decided to leave him in the shed forever. There was nothing and nobody who could stop him, nothing that he would not be capable of.

Eventually, Kingshaw crawled on his hands and knees back over the concrete and the mucky straw, on to the sacks. He pulled out the bottom ones, which were the dampest, and started to spread the others over the floor. He meant to lie down. He could see nothing at all, only feel clumsily at what he was doing. Then, something ran out of the sacks over his hands. He screamed, and began to beat them desperately against his trousers, terrified of what it might be. In the end, he was certain that it had gone. His fingers, when he opened them out again, were slimy and sticky.

He retched, and then began to vomit, all over the sacks, the sick coming down his nose and choking him. It tasted bitter. He bent forwards, holding his stomach. When it finished, he wiped his mouth on the sleeve of his shirt. He was shivering again.

There were no more sacks, only a pile of the straw, matted up in the corner nearest the door. Kingshaw groped his way to it. When he lay down, he pulled his knees tight up to his belly. He wanted to cry and couldn't. He put his hands up over his eyes, and behind the closed lids, green and red patterns heaved about, pricked out with the fine, bright points of stars.

In the end, he slept.

Susan Hill, *I'm the King of the Castle*

Puzzles

All these people showed great courage in their lives. On the next page there is one jumbled sentence about each of them. Write down the letter of the picture and then the correct sentence that describes it.

A

B

◄ E

C

D

Jumbled sentences

1 girl her who was experiences to kept a hide Jewish from and describing the diary Nazis a She had
2 the followers herself was Ancient who defeated her Romans but She killed was led an Briton against and
3 helping so in his handicapped was Britain people He wounded was Battle pilot life a to he very the but fighter badly devoted of
4 the wanted first he failed He died to Pole to be reach South safety man could the he reach but and before
5 devoted life better She her making for in life to women prison

Word study

These words occur in this unit. The number after each tells you the page it is on.
settlements 4
machete 4
infection 5
seamstress 7
boycott 7
humiliated 8
retaliatory 9
matted 12

1 Find each word and read the sentence it is in.
2 Write each word and against it write what you think it means.
3 If you do not know any of the words try to work out what it means from the sentence.
4 When you have written something for each word look them *all* up in the dictionary.
5 Write the correct meanings of any that you got wrong.

THE DAYS OF OUR LIVES

What's the first thing you remember?

The first thing that comes into my head, you mean?

No - the FIRST thing you remember...

Ah.. No, it's no good, it's gone. It was a long time ago..

You don't get my meaning. What is the first thing after all the things you've forgotten?

Oh, I see.... I've forgotten the question..

Calman

What is the first thing *you* remember?
Can you remember what your first day at school was like?
Can you remember anything before you first went to school?

Doodlebugs

During the Second World War the Germans sent unmanned aeroplanes with jet engines over Britain. By modern standards these missiles flew quite slowly and could be seen as they flew overhead. People in Britain found these attacks frightening because they could never tell when they were coming. The missiles were nicknamed Doodlebugs, because of the noise they made. Leslie Thomas lived for part of the war in an orphanage in a place that was heavily attacked by doodlebugs. It was run by a man the boys in the orphanage called the Gaffer.

In the empty hours of one night I lay sleepless in my bed in the corner of the dormitory and listened to the slow grind of an aeroplane. I listened idly, sliding my hands out of the bedclothes and stretching them up to the cool iron of the bedrail behind my head. The mounds that were the other boys breathed in undulating rows, someone stirred and turned and there was a boy snoring at the far end.

Abruptly the voice of the plane stopped. There were ten seconds or more of drifting silence. I lay unworried, but wondering why it should cut like that. Then, far away, but clear, came an explosion.

Flashes like wings of big white birds flew across the dormitory. Guns began to bite into the dark outside and behind their barrage the air-raid siren sounded. In the bed opposite little Tommy O'Connor, the smallest boy in the home, leapt upright, yellow hair standing on end, and began frantically to feel for his glasses on the locker.

The other kids were tumbling out of the blankets, pulling on their boots and overcoats. Boz, who, once he was asleep was well asleep, half rolled and then shouted irritably: 'Shut the bleeding row, will you! Can't anybody get any kip!'

I pulled him out on to the floor and he woke up. Then I clattered down the back stone stairs with the rest, out into the crashing night, and down the hole in the ground to the air-raid shelters. The shelter was long and ghostly and hung with damp. But it was a good place to be. We heard another hoarse engine overhead, the same cut-out, the protracted, ominous silence, then, much nearer this time, the explosion.

All night the guns were thumping and we heard the strong, uninterrupted engines of our own hunting planes while we crouched in the damp and the dark.

The summer morning came early and the birds sang with

delirious stupidity in the grey trees as we crawled out of our refuge. The first night of the flying-bombs, the sinister doodlebugs, was over. But they returned quickly.

It was a Saturday, I believe, and the Gaffer wouldn't let anyone out of the place, although we wanted to go swimming. About three in the afternoon a wicked shadow swooped out of the clear sun. Like a bird it fell, but nobody could run before it swept across the tower, missing it by a wingtip, and then exploded on the golf course a hundred yards away.

I was in the dining hall and Marlow, the Gaffer's assistant master, was walking through. He glanced out of the window and saw the falling shadow.

'Down!' he cried out. 'Everybody down!'

There were about twenty kids there just then. I was quick. I bounced on the floor, under a table, just as the impact of the explosion came. One of the floorboards came up and smacked me in the face. The shudder shattered the windows, flung the doors open, and resurrected the dust of ages in a choking cloud from the floor.

The bombs flew every day and night. The Gaffer, ancient and brave, used to come tearing across through the shrapnel and the hideous noises, his tin hat on the side of his head. He would fall down the entrance to the shelter and then, peering into the gloom, make sure we were all accounted for.

Then he would growl: 'If I catch anyone outside he'll be for it.'

Out he would go into the danger and run on his elderly legs to another shelter.

What a man this was. He was a hard old fellow, but he had his own ideas about duty and responsibility. At an age when he ought to have been down in Cornwall growing flowers or rhubarb, he had the lives of a hundred and fifty ragtag kids in his hands. He would have perished willingly, I know, rather than have had any harm come to the roughest, rowdiest young criminal under his care.

Leslie Thomas, *This Time Tomorrow*

Questions to think and talk about	
1	What were Leslie Thomas' thoughts and feelings as the first doodlebug approached?
2	What effect did the explosion have on the boys in the dormitory?
3	Why wouldn't the Gaffer let them out on the Saturday?
4	What was the usual pattern of a doodlebug attack?
5	What impression do you get of the Gaffer?

Writing Leslie Thomas wrote this description long after the war was over. Yet he remembered and told his story vividly and excitingly. Choose a memory that is still clear and strong in your mind. Describe it so that someone else can share it in the way that you shared Leslie Thomas' memories of the war.

Evacuation 1939–1945

For anyone born before 1940, a vivid early memory is of life during a world war. People born between 1925 and 1940 may well have been 'evacuated'.

For more than a million children who lived in large industrial cities and major ports throughout the British Isles, the outbreak of war meant a separation from their home and family. These children lived in the areas most likely to suffer heavy bombing, so the Government urged their parents to send them to the country where they would be safe. Some children returned home after only a few weeks or months, but others stayed in their country foster homes for the whole six years of the war.

Those who were lucky enough to have relatives or friends in the safe areas went to live with them, but most children were evacuated by the government. Very young children went away with their mothers, but children of school age usually went together as a school.

The children lined up in the school playground wearing special armbands or labels for identification. Each carried a gas mask case over his shoulder, and a small suitcase or bag containing clothes.

Teachers and special helpers marched the children down to the bus or railway station and travelled with them.

Sometimes the journey was very long and exhausting, and not even the teachers knew where they would end up. Each child was given a stamped postcard to send home to let his anxious parents know where he was.

Billeting officers had gone round homes in safe areas to list the ones that had room to take children. Normally, as the children arrived they were driven off by the billeting officers in ones and twos and deposited at their billet. In some areas, however, local people went to the station to meet the evacuees and pick the ones they wanted.

This was not a very good way of finding homes for children. The nicely dressed or pretty children were chosen first and it was very upsetting for the few who were left until last.

Many of the evacuated children came from poor homes in overcrowded areas of large cities. But the country people who had a room to spare were often those with a large house and a high standard of living.

The evacuees were often very nervous and unhappy in their strange new surroundings. They missed the friendly bustle of a large family, city cinemas and fish and chip shops, as well as some of their old friends.

Local children did not always get on well with the newcomers, referring to them as 'the invading hordes', or 'the vackees' and blaming them for any damage that was done.

Teachers had to sort out the problems of children who were unhappy in their billets and generally be like parents to them. It must have been a great strain on the teachers. One girl remembers that out of the staff evacuated with her girls' school, 'One committed suicide, one died of a heart attack, and one had a nervous breakdown, all within the space of a year.'

E. Allen, *Wartime Children 1939–45*

Questions

1 Which children were evacuated?
2 How did they travel?
3 Who went with them?
4 How did the children's parents find out where they had gone?
5 Who normally decided where the children would stay?
6 What was another way of deciding this?
7 What was the main difference between the houses that many of the children came *from* and those they often went *to*?
8 In what other ways were their new surroundings strange?
9 What did their teachers have to do?
10 What effect did it sometimes have on them?

All changed

*Charlie Smith was a petty criminal who spent much of his life in prison.
This is part of the story of what happened to him on one occasion when he
was released, after serving a six-year sentence. He arrived in London with
nowhere to go and no one to turn to.*

Wait a minute, he'd known a feller, hadn't he, used to live down
that way a few years back? Not far from the Elephant, down that
street round the back, off to the left. Been to his house once, nice
feller, what was his name, Ginger, Ginger something. He might let
him stay with him a night or two if he knew he'd just come out,
'course he would.

But Ginger what, what was his name, Ginger something,
Ginger what? Meredith, was it? No, it wasn't that. Drew, Ginger
Drew? No, it wasn't that either. Why should he think that? 'Course,
that was it, it was biscuits he was thinking of, ginger biscuits, they
made biscuits, that was why he was thinking of it.

Anyway, it didn't matter, because he could find the place all
right, knew where it was exactly. In that street round the back off to
the left. Know the house as soon as he saw it, been there before,
know it straight away. Even if he didn't, he could always ask which
was his house. Everybody'd know him, sure to, big chap with
bright red hair called Ginger, everybody'd be sure to know.

He went down the Underground, and bought himself a ticket.
Soon after quarter past ten he came up the steps at the Elephant and
Castle.

He found himself in an unknown country.

There were piles of earth, and excavation pits. Barriers and
hoardings and planks. Girders, barriers, fences. Bulldozers, cranes,
pile-drivers, trucks, bricks, concrete, sand. A featureless, desolate
land. Every building and street he had known was gone, flattened,
knocked down, disappeared. There was now only the outline of a
huge new traffic roundabout beginning to grow.

He stood. He looked. The scene was undecipherable. He
walked across the road and stepped over some drainage piping, then
turned round to see which way he had come, in case it helped. It
didn't. Then he saw by the edge of a shored-up cavity a young chap
in overalls sitting in the seat of a dumper-truck, having a smoke. He
went across to him.

'Know where they've gone, son?'

'Where who's gone, mate?'

'The people? All the people that used to live round about here?'

'Don't ask me, mate, how the hell'd I know where they've gone! Went years ago, I should think – rehousing and all that lark, know what I mean?'

He nodded, walked away. The boy shouted after him, laughing:

'Eh! We looked very careful before we knocked the houses down, made sure no one was still in!'

Tony Parker, *The Unknown Citizen*

Poem memories

Blackberry-picking

For Philip Hobsbaum

Late August, given heavy rain and sun
For a full week, the blackberries would ripen.
At first, just one, a glossy purple clot
Among others, red, green, hard as a knot.
You ate that first one and its flesh was sweet
Like thickened wine: summer's blood was in it
Leaving stains upon the tongue and lust for
Picking. Then red ones inked up and that hunger
Sent us out with milk-cans, pea-tins, jam-pots
Where briars scratched and wet grass bleached our boots.
Round hayfields, cornfields and potato-drills
We trekked and picked until the cans were full,
Until the tinkling bottom had been covered
With green ones, and on top big dark blobs burned
Like a plate of eyes. Our hands were peppered
With thorn pricks, our palms sticky as Bluebeard's.

We hoarded the fresh berries in the byre.
But when a bath was filled we found a fur,
A rat-grey fungus, glutting on our cache.
The juice was stinking too. Once off the bush
The fruit fermented, the sweet flesh would turn sour.
I always felt like crying. It wasn't fair
That all the lovely canfuls smelt of rot.
Each year I hoped they'd keep, knew they would not.

Seamus Heaney

Aunt Sue's Stories

Aunt Sue has a head full of stories.
Aunt Sue has a whole heart full of stories.
Summer nights on the front porch
Aunt Sue cuddles a brown-faced child to her bosom
And tells him stories.

Black slaves
Working in the hot sun,
And black slaves
Walking in the dewy night,
And black slaves
Singing sorrow songs on the banks of a mighty river
Mingle themselves softly
In the flow of old Aunt Sue's voice,
Mingle themselves softly
In the dark shadows that cross and recross
Aunt Sue's stories.

And the dark-faced child, listening,
Knows that Aunt Sue's stories are real stories.
He knows that Aunt Sue never got her stories
Out of any book at all,
But that they came
Right out of her own life.

The dark-faced child is quiet
Of a summer night
Listening to Aunt Sue's stories.

Langston Hughes

Algebra lesson

Errol O'Connor was born in Jamaica. He started school there and then moved to England with his family. When he was at school in London he wrote an account of his early life in Jamaica. This is part of his description of what school was like.

'Today,' Miss Brown stated, 'we are gwine to learn somet'ing new . . . ALGEBRA . . . now pay attention to de blackboard, while me show yu all 'ow fe do dem.'

She turned to face the blackboard, holding a piece of chalk at the tips of her fingers. My eyes wandered around the two other classes, and the other teachers writing in silence. My eyes caught sight of some small birds, as I glanced through an open window. They were flying from the trees to the ground, pecking at the earth for the crumbs they saw. How could they peck up the crumbs at such speed, without eating pebbles as well, I thought. I began counting them, but was interrupted by a shout from Miss Brown.

'Yes Miss,' I answered, absentmindedly.

'Come out and show de class 'ow to do dis sum,' she said calmly, knowing that I hadn't been paying any attention.

I didn't answer, I was too nervous. As she said 'come out,' I felt as if I was walking alone through a graveyard. I slowly moved towards the blackboard, wondering if she would hit me hard. I took the chalk from her and glanced at the strange-looking sum on the board. It was the first time I had seen anything like it.

a = 2, b = 4, c = 10, what is a x b + c. I read over and over again in my mind; but couldn't understand it. I tried to remember what she had said, but I couldn't.

'Me a go lick dem birds when me see dem . . . jus' let dem wait; a dem cause me fe no know 'ow fe do dis sums, let . . .'

My thoughts were rudely broken by the swish of the cane. Miss Brown hit me time and time again, before I knew where to run to. I slipped through the passage and reached my desk in half the time it took me on normal occasions. I had escaped from Miss Brown with a stinging back. I heard sniggering and laughing as tears rolled down my cheeks. My back was hurting as if it was on fire.

I took one quick glance through the open window to see the small birds. I thought of killing them all, if I could just catch them. Right through the day I felt the pain, digging into my back. Sheila Barnes continued to laugh after the lesson was finished, I felt like rubbing her ugly face in the dirt, but I dreaded getting another beating from Miss Brown.

School was over, and I was happy to leave. I hated Miss Brown for hitting me so hard on my first day back to school. I wished that I didn't have to go back to school, as Ricky and I headed for home.

'Miss Brown lick yu 'ard today, eh,' Ricky said, smiling as we walked home.

'Me was more frighten dan ant'ing else, de way de cane stuck ina me back, frighten bad, bad bwoy, dats why me almost cry . . .'

'Wey you mean yu almost cry? . . . y'eye wata run down yu cheek like a river,' Ricky laughed.

'A de chalk get in a me y'eye man,' I answered.

'De chalk neva come nowey near yu y'eye . . . it was miles off, so no try fe trick me, cause me is a bigger jinnal★ dan you,' Ricky continued to laugh.

''Ow yu fe see me y'eye when yu was an de 'rang side?' I added.

'Me lean ova,' Ricky answered, in a serious, convincing voice.

'Wey yu mean, yu lean ova?'

'Jus' wey me say.'

'Yu coulda lean straight across de class room yu still couldn't see wata in a me y'eye,' I replied.

'Bwoy 'ow yu a go notice everyt'ing so, when Miss Brown was a drap some licks pan yu bac' . . . an yu was a run so fas' you never have time fe look pan me,' Ricky said.

'Me jus' see dat yu wasn't looking pan me, a so me say,' I argued.

'Man me say you cry, so yu cry, and dats fact,' said Ricky, with a deep breath.

I said nothing more about my beating and neither did Ricky. I could still feel the pain slightly and that was enough for one day.

Errol O'Connor, *Jamaica Child*

★ jinnal: a crafty, sly or cunning person

Errol O' Connor has written the dialogue in Jamaican Creole. Most Creole words are English but some come from languages spoken in West Africa, the original home of black Jamaican people. Creole pronunciation and grammar differ from standard English.
me means *I* as well as *me.*
fe means *to* or *for*
the sound 'th' does not exist in Creole

Any Saturday in 1920

Saturday was the happiest day of our life. We got our Saturday penny and our favourite dinner – fish and chips.

Now, we had to earn this penny. In the first place we had to behave ourselves for a week. In the second place we all had our various jobs to do, Saturday morning, very quietly, because Dad was a London taxi driver and he worked at night and slept during the day. So all our jobs had to be done on tip-toe.

Now, my Dad was a huge man. He weighed 17½ stone of muscle, and in his younger days had been an amateur wrestling instructor. But he was what I called a gentle giant. He never smacked one of us kids once, although he could have snapped us over his knee. He used to shout and could he swear. But he never hit us.

So Saturday morning arrives. Now, if you've ever seen a tin of sardines you'll know how we slept: three girls at the top, two boys at the bottom, the baby in a drawer in Mum's room with Mum and Dad. We only had two rooms and a very tiny kitchen. So, as you can imagine, when we got our Dad in there weighing 17½ stones there wasn't any room for anybody or anything else. In any case there was only room for a large table and two chairs. Now, we got up early Saturday, because if you got your jobs done in time you had your penny and you went to the penny rush. Now, the penny rush was pictures. We used to see a film and a serial with Pearl White in it every week – that is if you got your jobs done in time. When you went to the cinema, which was called the Central Hall, you had either an orange, a bag of sweets or a pencil given to you; but if you made a row when you got inside, you got a clump round the earhole and were slung out (HA)! Needless to say, being the eldest, I rarely went because I had too many jobs to do. But we used to send Jacky so he could take Jimmy in his arms and we could get rid of at least one noise.

Now, my job was the outside lavatory. It was shared by us six kids and Mum and Dad and the family of five upstairs. It was my job to clean it, scrub the wooden top, whitewash the sides, and scrub the floor. There was no toilet roll in those days. So, while I was doing this, Jacky was tearing up the newspapers for the week, making a hole in the corner, and putting the string through to tie up in the lavatory in place of a toilet roll.

Now, my Dad was a great gambler – he gambled every day of his life except Sundays. So there was a lot of newspapers: he bought all the newspapers under the sun. So there was always a ton of toilet paper, as we called it. Well, we didn't call it toilet paper, but I mustn't tell you what we did call it. Well, we used to call it bum paper. And God help Jacky if the bum paper ran out.

Now in our yard my Dad kept a goat, a nanny goat, who at the time was pregnant. He thought us kids would drink the milk. He also kept chickens and he also bred greyhounds. This was in Hackney, London. Nanny had two kids. My Dad was midwife. He came rushing in when the first one was born, which was fawn, and rushing in after the second one was born, which was black and white. Well, us kids would not drink the milk. My Dad was the milkmaid. He looked charming sitting out there in the yard. And all the neighbours used to get on their walls to look at him. And anyhow none of us kids would drink the milk because it was a dark yellow and we were used to skimmed milk. It's true – on my honour. If I should die this minute, it's true. Dad called us every name you could think of. But I noticed he never drank it himself. But the man next door, named Mr Ryde, who was dying from what in those days we called consumption, drank quite a lot of it, so it didn't all go to waste.

Now to Saturday. Jacky's done his bum paper and he's taken Jimmy to the pictures. He's got his Saturday penny. Winnie has the knives and forks to clean – there was nothing stainless in those days. The forks and the spoons were cleaned with a metal polish which was called 'Bluebell', and the knives were cleaned on a knife board with some stuff that was called 'Monkey Brand'. It cost one penny and lasted almost a year, and God 'elp you if you didn't make it last a year. Anyway, that was Winnie's job. Charlie had all the greengrocery to get because he was a big boy for his age. He was eleven and he had the greengrocery to get and the chickens' house to clean out, which was cleaned out once a week.

Mum used to go to the market – Ridley Road market – while all this was going on. Now after I'd cleaned the lavatory and scrubbed the passage right through, and cleaned inside and outside of the windows (which wasn't very many as we only had three rooms), my next job was to go and get our Saturday dinner, which was the favourite. A tuppenny and a penn'orth each – a tuppenny piece of fish which you would now pay five bob for, and a penn'orth of chips, which would easy cost two bob today. And there were no plates to wash because we ate 'em out of a newspaper. It was absolutely lovely, we thoroughly enjoyed it.

Saturday night was bath night, which I hated. Not because I hated a bath, but it was the way it had to be done. It was such a small kitchen that the bath was hanging up on a nail out in the yard – a tin bath. But it was such a small kitchen that it wouldn't go on the floor between the fireplace and the table. So it had to go on the table. And next door's kitchen overlooked our kitchen, and they could see us all having our bath, which I did not like. Now we started with Phyllis who was the luckiest of all because she had clean water and the only two clean towels we had. Mum used to have the big iron saucepans on top of the hob, getting hotter all the time. My job was to dry them as they came out. We went in numbers, Phyllis first. It was very hard to dry Phyllis as she was partially paralysed and used to have a very bad temper. We had no nighties or pyjamas. We put our clean vest on and went and sat on the bed in the back room. Because this was the night when we had a cup of cocoa, the only night of the week. Next comes Jacky, who was always as black as your hat. And the water is now getting slightly discoloured. Also another saucepan of water goes in – hot water – and the towels are getting a bit damp. I dry Jacky, and so forth, till it gets to Charlie. Now, by this time, the two towels are soaking wet. So Charlie has to dry himself on the others' dirty underclothes.

Now comes ME. I kick up a stink because I don't want to stand on the table because the Wrights next door could see me. I used to get a wallop on my bare behind for a start. Another saucepan of water would go in and I now got in to a pale grey soup. I had to wash my hair, which was very long, in this. We all had to wash our hair in this. And eventually I had two wet towels, everybody's wet underclothes, and my own dry underclothes, to dry on.

Then came the performance of emptying the bath. So we all had to get hold of an end here – Mum got hold of one end, because she was as strong as a lion. You notice I call her Mum. I've always called her Mum. She's still alive today – she's 85. Mum got hold of one end of the bath. We used to scramble out, in our vests, to the backyard, to empty the bath down the drain, and hang it up again on the wall out in the yard. Now we come in, and we're all sitting in our vests, very dignified I must say. But as I say, there were no nighties, and there were no pyjamas. And then we had a cup of Perks's cocoa. Now this was three ha'pence a quarter, and to us kids it was marvellous, 'cos we had condensed milk in it.

Then we all went to bed in the same way as we got out. Phyllis by the wall up the top, Jacky at the bottom with his feet in Phyllis' mouth, and me being the eldest, I was up the top on the end. I spent more time falling out of bed in those days than I've done in the whole of my life put together! And thus ended the happiest day of our lives – Saturday in 1920.

Lil Smith, *The Good Old Bad Old Days*

Puzzles

Evacuees

In this story, five sentences have been left out and the gaps have been
closed up. Read the story and try to work out where the sentences
have been missed out. They are listed in the wrong order on the next
page.
   The story tells what happened when one lot of evacuees arrived at
their destination.

'Stand by there, then,' the woman said. 'There by the wall with the
others, and someone will choose you.'
   Carrie looked round, bewildered, and saw Albert Sandwich.
She whispered, 'What's happening?' and he said, 'A kind of cattle
5   auction, it seems.'②
   He gave Carrie her suitcase, then marched to the end of the hall,
sat down on his own, and took a book out of his pocket.
   Carrie wished she could do that⑤But she had already begun to
feel ill with shame at the fear that no one would choose her, the way
10   she always felt when they picked teams at school.⑥She dragged Nick
(her brother) into the line of waiting children and stood, eyes on the
ground, hardly daring to breathe. When someone called out, 'A nice
little girl for Mrs Davies, now,' she felt she would suffocate. She
looked up but unfocused her eyes so that passing faces blurred and
15   swam in front of her.   ①
   Nick's hand tightened in hers. No one would take home a boy
who looked like that, so pale and delicate. They would think he was
bound to get ill, and be a trouble to them. She said in a low, fierce
voice, 'Why don't you smile and look nice,' and he blinked with
20   surprise, looking so small and so sweet that she softened. She said,
'Oh it's all right, I'm not cross. I won't leave you.'
   Minutes passed, feeling like hours. Children left the line and
were taken away.③She and Nick, and a few tough-looking boys, and
an ugly girl with a squint who had two little sisters. And Albert
25   Sandwich who was still sitting quietly on his suitcase, reading his
book and taking no notice. *He* didn't care! Carrie tossed her head
and hummed under her breath to show she didn't either.

Nina Bawden, *Carrie's War*

Missing sentences

1 She looked at his white face and wanted to shake him.
2 He sounded calmly disgusted.
3 Only unwanted ones left, Carrie thought.
4 Suppose she was left to the last!
5 Sit down and read as if nothing else mattered.

Word study

These words occur in this unit. The number after each one tells you the page it is on.

billet   19
undecipherable   20
cavity   20
cache   22
fermented   22
midwife   27
consumption   27

1 Find each word and read the sentence it is in.
2 Write each word on a new line, and against it, write what you think it means. If you are not sure, try to work out what it means from the sentence.
3 Look *all* the words up in the dictionary.
4 Write the correct meanings of any that you got wrong.

ALL WINTER LONG

In which country do you think each of these photographs was taken?
What would winter be like in each of these places?
Do you like winter as a season?

Indian warning

In this story all the paragraphs except the first have been printed in the wrong order. What is the correct order of the paragraphs?

1 One afternoon a little crowd of men gathered in Harthorn's store in town. The trains, which had been stopped by the blizzard, were running again, and men had come in to town from their claims to buy some groceries and hear the news.

2 They all looked at him and did not say anything.
'You white men,' he said. 'I tell-um you.'
He showed seven fingers again. 'Big snow.' Again, seven fingers. 'Big snow.' Again seven fingers. '*Heap* big snow, many moons.'

3 He was a very old Indian. His brown face was carved in deep wrinkles and shrivelled on the bones, but he stood tall and straight. His arms were folded under a grey blanket, holding it wrapped around him. His head was shaved to a scalp-lock and an eagle's feather stood up from it. His eyes were bright and sharp. Behind him the sun was shining on the dusty street and an Indian pony stood there waiting.

4 Royal and Almanzo Wilder had come from their homesteads, Almanzo driving his own fine team of matched Morgans, the best team in all that country. Mr. Boast was there, standing in the middle of the little crowd and setting it laughing when he laughed. Pa had walked in with his gun on his arm, but he had not seen so much as a jackrabbit, and now he was waiting while Mr. Harthorn weighed the piece of salt pork that he had had to buy instead.

5 No one heard a footstep, but Pa felt that someone was behind him and he turned to see who it was. Then suddenly Mr. Boast stopped talking. All the others looked to see what Mr. Boast saw, and they stood up quickly from the cracker boxes and the plough. Almanzo slid down from the counter. Nobody said anything.

6 Then he tapped his breast with his forefinger. 'Old! Old! I have seen!' he said proudly.
He walked out of the store to his waiting pony and rode away towards the west.
'Well, I'll be jiggered,' Mr. Boast said.

7 'What was that about seven big snows?' Almanzo asked. Pa told him. The Indian meant that every seventh winter was a hard winter and that at the end of three times seven years came the hardest winter of all. He had come to tell the white men that this coming winter was a twenty-first winter, that there would be seven months of blizzards.

'You suppose the old geezer knows what he's talking about?' Royal wanted to know. No one could answer that.

8   'Heap big snow come,' this Indian said.

The blanket slid on his shoulder and one naked brown arm came out. It moved in a wide sweep, to north, to west, to east, and gathered them all together and swirled.

'Heap big snow, big wind,' he said.

'How long?' Pa asked him.

'Many moons,' the Indian said. He held up four fingers, then three fingers. Seven fingers, seven months; blizzards for seven months.

9   It was only an Indian, but somehow the sight of him kept them all quiet. He stood there and looked at them, at Pa, at Mr. Boast, at Royal Wilder and each of the other men, and finally at Almanzo.

Laura Ingalls Wilder, *The Long Winter*

Questions to think and talk about

1   In what country and at what time is the story set?
2   Why should the men be so concerned about heavy blizzards?
3   Do *you* 'suppose the old geezer knows what he's talking about'?
4   Do you think the men would be likely to take any notice of what the Indian said?
5   If they did, what preparations could they make?

Writing

You are one of the men in the story. When the Indian has gone, you ride back to your homestead and tell your family what happened and what you think of it. Write the conversation.

1,4,5,9,3,8,2,6,7 ✓ Good

excellent

Avalanche

Avalanches are quite common in the Alps and other mountainous areas of the world. The mountain may look perfectly peaceful, blanketed in snow. Underneath the surface, however, the snow may be unstable. A change in weather conditions, bringing slightly warmer temperatures, can be very dangerous. The snow beneath the surface begins to melt. This in turn means that the snow on top is no longer safely 'fixed' to the rock of the mountain.

A sudden noise, a slight vibration, and the avalanche begins. Once it has started it gathers more and more snow and more and more speed. Anything in its path is carried along and finally buried, many feet beneath the surface.

Countries like Switzerland, which suffer badly from avalanches, have special rescue teams. They can be moved quickly to the scene of an avalanche to begin the job of rescuing those who have been buried by the snow. They use dogs to smell out where people are buried. They also use fine probes which are pushed gently into the snow. When they meet resistance it may be a body.

When a victim has been located, the men dig carefully to free him as quickly as possible. If a victim is not rescued within about half an hour his chances of survival are not very good.

True or false?

1 Avalanches only happen in mountainous areas.
2 A mountain that looks safe from avalanches may not be.
3 Avalanches start when all the snow melts.
4 Avalanches are caused by rocks falling.
5 Avalanches can be started by noise.
6 Once an avalanche has started, its speed increases.
7 Rescue teams always travel by helicopter.
8 Dogs are used to detect people buried in the snow.
9 Probes are used to see if the victims are still alive.
10 After half an hour all the victims are dead.

The Warrior of Winter

He met the star his enemy
   They fought the woods leafless.
He gripped his enemy.
   They trampled fields to quag★.
His enemy was stronger.
   A star fought against him.

He fought his losing fight
   Up to the neck in the river.
Grimly he fought in gateways,
   He struggled among stones.
He left his strength in puddles.
   The star grew stronger.

Rising and falling
   He blundered against houses.
He gurgled for life in ditches.
   Clouds mopped his great wounds.
His shattered weapons glittered.
   The star gazed down..

Wounded and prisoner
   He slept on rotten sacking.
He gnawed bare stalks and turnip tops
   In the goose's field.
The sick sheep froze beside him.
   The star was his guard.

With bones like frozen plumbing
   He lay in the blue morning.
His teeth locked in his head
   Like the trap-frozen fox.
But he rejoiced a tear in the sun.
   Like buds his dressings softened.

Ted Hughes

★ quag, quagmire: soft, wet, muddy ground

The Mother's Song

It is so still in the house,
There is a calm in the house;
The snowstorm wails out there,
And the dogs are rolled up with snouts under the tail.
My little boy is sleeping on the ledge,
On his back he lies, breathing through his open mouth.
His little stomach is bulging round –
Is it strange if I start to cry with joy?

Eskimo poem

Three Haiku

I could eat it!
The snow that falls
    So softly, so softly.

There are thanks to be given:
This snow on the bed quilt –
    It too is from Heaven.

Snow melts
And the village is overflowing –
    With children.

Kobayashi Issa

Thaw

Over the land freckled with snow half-thawed
The speculating rooks at their nests cawed
And saw from elm-tops, delicate as flowers of grass,
What we below could not see, Winter pass.

Edward Thomas

Fire on Christmas Eve

It was on the afternoon of the day of Christmas Eve, and I was in Mrs Prothero's garden, waiting for cats, with her son Jim. It was snowing. Patient, cold, and callous, our hands wrapped in socks, we waited to snowball the cats. The wise cats never appeared. We were so still that we never heard Mrs Prothero's first cry from her igloo at the bottom of the garden. But soon the voice grew louder. 'Fire!' cried Mrs Prothero, and she beat the dinner-gong. And we ran down the garden, with the snowballs in our arms, towards the house, and smoke, indeed, was pouring out of the dining-room, and the gong was bombilating, and Mrs Prothero was announcing ruin like a town-crier in Pompeii. This was better than all the cats in Wales standing on the wall in a row. We bounded into the house, laden with snow-balls, and stopped at the open door of the smoke-filled room. Something was burning all right; perhaps it was Mr Prothero, who always slept there after midday dinner with a newspaper over his face; but he was standing in the middle of the room, saying 'A fine Christmas!' and smacking at the smoke with a slipper.

'Call the fire-brigade,' cried Mrs Prothero as she beat the gong.

'They won't be there,' said Mr Prothero, 'it's Christmas.'

There was no fire to be seen, only clouds of smoke and Mr Prothero standing in the middle of them, waving his slipper as though he were conducting.

'Do something,' he said.

And we threw all our snowballs into the smoke – I think we missed Mr Prothero – and ran out of the house to the phone box.

'Let's call the police as well,' Jim said.

'And the ambulance.'

'And Ernie Jenkins, he likes fires.'

But we only called the fire-brigade, and soon the fire-engine came and three tall men in helmets brought a hose into the house and Mr Prothero got out just in time before they turned it on. Nobody could have had a noisier Christmas Eve. And when the firemen turned off the hose and were standing in the wet and smoky room, Jim's aunt, Miss Prothero, came downstairs and peered in at them. Jim and I waited, very quietly, to hear what she would say to them. She said the right thing, always. She looked at the three tall firemen in their shining helmets, standing among the smoke and cinders and dissolving snowballs, and she said: 'Would you like something to read?'

Dylan Thomas, *Quite Early One Morning*

Alone on the trail

Day had broken cold and gray, exceedingly cold and gray, when the man had turned aside from the main Yukon trail and climbed the high earth-bank where a dim and little-travelled trail led eastward through the fat spruce timberland. It was a steep bank, and he paused for breath at the top, excusing the act to himself by looking at his watch. It was nine o'clock. There was no sun nor hint of sun, though there was not a cloud in the sky. It was a clear day and yet there seemed a subtle gloom that made the day dark. This fact did not worry the man. He was used to the lack of sun.

The man flung a look back along the way he had come. The Yukon lay a mile wide and hidden under three feet of ice. On top of this ice were as many feet of snow. It was all pure white, rolling in gentle undulations where the ice jams of the freeze-up had formed. North and south, as far as his eye could see, it was unbroken white, save for a dark hairline that curved and twisted from around the spruce-covered island to the north, where it disappeared behind another spruce-covered island. This dark hairline was the trail.

But all this – the mysterious, far-reaching hairline trail, the absence of sun from the sky, the tremendous cold, and the strangeness and weirdness of it all – made no impression on the man. It was not because he was long used to it. He was a newcomer in the land and this was his first winter. The trouble with him was that he was without imagination. He was quick and alert in the things of life, but only in the things, and not in the significances. Fifty degrees below zero meant eighty-odd degrees of frost. Such fact impressed him as being cold and uncomfortable, and that was all. It did not lead him to meditate upon his frailty as a creature of temperature, and upon man's frailty in general, able only to live within certain narrow limits of heat and cold. Fifty degrees below zero stood for a bite of frost that hurt and must be guarded against by the use of mittens, ear flaps, warm moccasins, and thick socks. Fifty degrees below zero was to him just precisely fifty degrees below zero. That there should be anything more to it than that was a thought that never entered his head.

As he turned to go on, he spat speculatively. There was a sharp, explosive crackle that startled him. He spat again. And again, in the air, before it could fall to the snow, the spittle crackled. He knew that at fifty below spittle crackled on the snow, but this spittle had crackled in the air. Undoubtedly it was colder than fifty below – how much colder he did not know. But the temperature did not

matter. He would be in to camp by six o'clock; a bit after dark, it was true, but the boys would be there, a fire would be going, and a hot supper would be ready. As for lunch, he pressed his hand against the protruding bundle under his jacket. It was also under his shirt, wrapped up in a handkerchief and lying against the naked skin. It was the only way to keep the biscuits from freezing. He smiled agreeably to himself as he thought of those biscuits, each cut open and sopped in bacon grease, and each enclosing a generous slice of fried bacon.

He plunged in among the big spruce trees. The trail was faint. A foot of snow had fallen since the last sled had passed over, and he was glad he was without a sled, travelling light. In fact, he carried nothing but the lunch wrapped in the handkerchief. He was surprised, however, at the cold. It certainly was cold, he concluded, as he rubbed his numb nose and cheekbones with his mittened hand. He was a warm-whiskered man, but the hair on his face did not protect the high cheek-bones and the eager nose that thrust itself aggressively into the frosty air.

At the man's heels trotted a dog, a big native husky. The animal was depressed by the tremendous cold. It knew that it was no time for travelling. Its instinct told it a truer tale than was told to the man by the man's judgement. In reality, it was not merely colder than fifty below zero; it was colder than sixty below, than seventy below. It was seventy-five below zero. Since the freezing point is thirty-two above zero, it meant that one hundred and seven degrees of frost obtained. The dog did not know about thermometers. But the brute had its instinct. It experienced a vague but menacing apprehension that subdued it and made it slink along at the man's heels, and that made it question eagerly every unwonted movement of the man as if expecting him to go into camp or to seek shelter somewhere and build a fire. The dog had learned fire, and it wanted fire, or else to burrow under the snow and cuddle its warmth away from the air.

The frozen moisture of its breathing had settled on its fur in a fine powder of frost, and especially were its jowls, muzzle, and eyelashes whitened by its crystallized breath. The man's red beard and moustache were likewise frosted, but more solidly, the deposit taking the form of ice and increasing with every warm, moist breath he exhaled. Also the man was chewing tobacco, and the muzzle of ice held his lips so rigidly that he was unable to clear his chin when he expelled the juice. The result was that a crystal beard of the colour and solidity of amber was increasing its length on his chin. If he fell down it would shatter itself, like glass, into brittle fragments. But he did not mind.

He held on through the level stretch of woods for several miles, and dropped down a bank to the frozen bed of a small stream. This was Henderson Creek, and he knew he was ten miles from the forks. He looked at his watch. It was ten o'clock. He was making four miles an hour, and he calculated that he would arrive at the forks at half-past twelve. He decided to celebrate that event by eating his lunch there.

The dog dropped in again at his heels, with a tail drooping discouragement, as the man swung along the creek bed. The furrow of the old sled trail was plainly visible, but a dozen inches of snow covered the marks of the last runners. In a month no man had come up or down that silent creek. The man held steadily on. He was not much given to thinking, and just then particularly he had nothing to think about save that he would eat lunch at the forks and that at six o'clock he would be in camp with the boys.

Once in a while the thought reiterated itself that it was very cold and that he had never experienced such cold. As he walked along he rubbed his cheekbones and nose with the back of his mittened hand. He did this automatically, now and again changing hands. But, rub as he would, the instant he stopped his cheekbones went numb, and the following instant the end of his nose went numb. He was sure to frost his cheeks; he knew that. But it didn't matter much, after all. What were frosted cheeks? A bit painful, that was all; they were never serious.

Empty as the man's mind was of thoughts, he was keenly observant, and he noticed the changes in the creek, the curves and bends and timber jams, and always he sharply noted where he placed his feet. Once, coming round a bend, he shied abruptly, like a startled horse, curved away from the place where he had been walking, and retreated several paces back along the trail. The creek he knew was frozen clear to the bottom – but he also knew that there were springs that bubbled out from the hillsides and ran along under the snow and on top of the ice of the creek. He knew that the coldest snaps never froze these springs, and he knew likewise their danger. They were traps. They hid pools of water under the snow that might be three inches deep, or three feet. Sometimes a skin of ice half an inch thick covered them, and in turn was covered by the snow. Sometimes there were alternate layers of water and ice skin, so that when one broke through he kept on breaking through for a while, sometimes wetting himself to the waist.

That was why he had shied in such panic. He had felt the give under his feet and heard the crackle of a snow-hidden ice-skin. And to get his feet wet in such a temperature meant trouble and danger. At the very least it meant delay, for he would be forced to stop and build a fire, and under its protection to bare his feet while he dried his socks and moccasins. He reflected awhile, rubbing his nose and cheeks, then skirted to the left, stepping gingerly and testing the footing for each step. Once clear of the danger, he took a fresh chew of tobacco and swung along at his four-mile gait.

In the course of the next two hours he came upon several similar traps. Usually the snow above the hidden pools had a sunken, candied appearance that advertized the danger. Once again, however, he had a close call; and once, suspecting danger, he compelled the dog to go on in front. The dog did not want to go. It hung back until the man shoved it forward, and then it went quickly across the white, unbroken surface. Suddenly it broke through, floundered to one side, and got away to firmer footing. It had wet its forefeet and legs, and almost immediately the water that clung to it turned to ice. It made quick efforts to lick the ice off its legs, then dropped down in the snow and began to bite out the ice that had formed between the toes. This was a matter of instinct. To permit the ice to remain would mean sore feet. It did not know this. It merely obeyed the mysterious prompting that arose from the deep crypts of its being. But the man knew, having achieved a judgement on the subject, and he removed the mitten from his right hand and helped tear out the ice particles. He did not expose his fingers more than a minute, and was astonished at the swift numbness that smote them. It certainly was cold. He pulled on the mitten hastily, and beat the hand savagely across his chest.

At half-past twelve, to the minute, he arrived at the forks of the creek. He was pleased at the speed he had made. If he kept it up he would certainly be with the boys by six. He unbuttoned his jacket and shirt and drew forth his lunch. The action consumed no more than a quarter of a minute, yet in that brief moment the numbness laid hold of the exposed fingers. He did not put the mitten on, but, instead, struck the fingers a dozen sharp smashes against his leg. Then he sat down on a snow-covered log to eat. The sting that followed upon the striking of his fingers against his leg ceased so quickly that he was startled. He had no chance to take a bite of biscuit. He struck the fingers repeatedly and returned them to the mitten, baring the other hand for the purpose of eating. He tried to take a mouthful, but the ice muzzle prevented it. He had forgotten to build a fire and thaw out. He chuckled at his foolishness, and as he chuckled he noted the numbness creeping into the exposed fingers. Also he noted that the stinging which had first come to his toes when he sat down was already passing away. He wondered whether the toes were warm or numb. He moved them inside the moccasins and decided they were numb.

He pulled the mitten on hurriedly and stood up. He was a bit frightened.

Jack London, *To Build a Fire*

Puzzles

The Indian's warning

This is the continuation of the story at the beginning of the unit. A number of words have been missed out. Read the passage carefully and try to work out what they should be. Then write down the number of each blank and the word you think should go there.

'Just on the chance,' Royal said, '..*I*..¹.... say we move in to town ....²*for*.. the winter. My feed store beats ....³*a*.. claim shanty all hollow for wintering .....⁴*in* . We can stay back there till ⁵*spring*.. How'd it suit you, Manzo?'

'..*suits*.. me,' said Almanzo.

'How do you ...*feel*⁷.. about moving in to town, Boast?' ....⁸*Pa*.. asked.

Mr Boast slowly shook his ..*head*. 'Don't see how we could. We've ..*got*¹⁰... too much stock, cattle and horses, ..*and*¹¹.. chickens. There's no place in town ...¹²*to*.. keep them even if I could ..*afford*¹³ to pay the rent. We're fixed pretty ..*well*¹⁴ for the winter on the claim. ....¹⁵*I*. guess Ellie and I better stay ..*with*¹⁶. it.'

Everyone was sober. Pa paid ...*for*¹⁷.... his groceries and set out, walking *quickly*¹⁸ towards home. Now and then he *looked*¹⁹ back at the northwest sky. It ..*was*²⁰.. clear and the sun was shining.

...*Ma*²¹. was taking bread from the oven ..*when*²² Pa came in. Carrie and Grace ...*had*²³.. run to meet him; then came ....²⁴*in*... with him. Mary went on quietly *sewing*²⁵ but Laura jumped up.

'Is anything *wrong*²⁶ Charles?' Ma asked, tipping the good-smelling *loaves*²⁷ from the pan onto a clean *white*²⁸ cloth. 'You're home early.'

'Nothing's wrong,' ...*Pa*²⁹... answered. 'Here are your sugar and ..*tea*³⁰.. and a bit of salt pork. ....³¹*I*. didn't get a rabbit. Not a ..*thing*³² is wrong,' he repeated, 'but we're moving ..*to*³³.... town as quick as we can. I've *got*³⁴... to haul in hay, first, ..*to*³⁵... the stock. I can haul one ..*load*³⁶.. before dark if I hustle.'

'Goodness, ..*child*³⁷!' Ma gasped, but Pa was on ..*his*³⁸.. way to the stable. Carrie and ..*little*³⁹ Grace stared at Ma and at ....⁴⁰*Laura* and at Ma again. Laura looked ...*at*⁴¹. Ma and Ma looked helplessly at ..*her*⁴².

'Your Pa never did such a ..*thing*⁴³ before,' Ma said.

Word study

Each of these dictionary definitions refers to a word that occurs somewhere in this unit. The number after each definition tells you which page the word is on. What are the words?

1 Piece of land marked out for use by one man or his family.   32
2 House with outbuildings, farm.   32
3 Not steady in position.   34
4 Small but rapid to and fro movement, quivering.   34
5 Wet swampy ground.   36
6 Bumped into something clumsily.   36
7 Broken suddenly and violently in pieces.   36
8 Cover lying over bed-clothes, bedspread.   37
9 Having a guess about what may happen.   37
10 Wave-like motions or forms.   39

Clouds

People who study the weather name clouds according to their shapes. The words they use come from Latin:

cumulus = a mass or heap   *cirrus* = plume, curl
stratus = level, flat   *nimbus* = dark grey rain cloud
altus   = high

Match these cloud names to the pictures underneath:

A *altocumulus*   C *cumulus*
B *cirrocumulus*   D *cumulonimbus*

Highton News

No. 2341   January 22 1981   Weather forecast: more snow

SNOWED UP!

School Hit by Freak Blizzard

As freak weather conditions swept much of Britain today, Highton was struck by a freak blizzard. Gale force winds blew feet of snow onto the town in a matter of minutes.

NOTHING LIKE IT
'I've never seen anything like it,' declared 76-year-old road sweeper Albert James, who has lived in Highton all his life. 'It beats 1979 into a cocked hat.'

SCHOOL STRUCK
Worst hit was Highton's comprehensive school, on its out-of-town site on the edge of the moors. Within moments snow was six feet high against the walls of the school and the road was completely blocked.

ONLY ONE CLASS LEFT
Fortunately, most of the children had already been sent home by Headmaster William Hope. 'I heard the lunchtime forecast' he told me tonight, 'and decided to evacuate.' Unfortunately what Mr Hope did not know was that one class from the lower school was on its way *back* into the school – having returned from a visit to a nearby factory.

Little is known but it is assumed that this second-year class is now marooned inside the school building with the two teachers who took them to the factory.

Beginning

It is *your* school and *your* class that have been snowed up. In this project you are going to tell the story of what happens. It will take the form of a kind of diary.

To begin with you have to make a number of decisions about the class and the school. You can write about a real school and real people, or you can make them up.

The school Make a plan of the school showing where all the main parts are. There is no need to be too accurate or to show all the classrooms. But you should show the following:

your own classroom
canteen/dining hall and kitchens
craft workshops and artroom
domestic science and needlework rooms
gym
main entrances and exits
office(s) and telephone(s)

The class Whether it is your own class you are writing about, or a made-up one, give these details:

number of boys and girls
names of everyone in the class

Friends Choose two people in the class who are your friends. For each one write a 'personal dossier':

```
HELEN SPENCER

Height: 5'1"     Build: slim
Hair: light brown     Eyes: hazel
Special features: freckles

Helen is a cheerful and happy-go-
lucky person.  She likes the company
of other people and has lots of
friends.  She likes telling jokes,
but
```

Teachers Describe the two teachers who are with you.
If you write about real people, you must be fair, and be ready to show them what you have written about them.

Settling in

MR A: . . . and the telephones don't work, so we're completely cut off.

MISS B: So we shall have to spend the night here. We shall need bedding.

MR A: And some form of heating.

MISS B: Then there's food to be got . . .

MR A: And cleared away afterwards.

MISS B: Separate dormitories for girls and boys.

MR A: Arrangements for washing.

MISS B: There's a lot to be done, so let's get started.

Thinking   Think how these needs could be supplied in your school:

Where is the food and can you get at it?
How can it be cooked?
What about beds and bedding?
Which are the best rooms for sleeping?
How would you be able to keep warm?
    and so on . . .

Writing   Write a description of how the teachers and class organize themselves and overcome these problems.

What's for supper?

It is getting late in the day and the time has come to prepare a meal.

Thinking

Decide on a menu for: cooked supper tonight
breakfast
a main meal tomorrow

How many people have to be fed? *24*

Look at the picture. It shows you the food that is available in the school kitchen. What food will you use for each meal?

How much of each do you need? *24*

How is each part of the meal prepared? *Stove*

salad
crackers
steak
jelb

Writing

Write down:

1 The menu for: cooked supper
breakfast
tomorrow's main meal.

2 A list of the food you need for each.

3 The recipe(s) for either supper or the main meal.

Pancakes
bread

salad
cheese
chicken
ice cream

Bedtime

Writing Imagine how you would feel as you went to bed on that first night. Write a poem describing the thoughts that pass through your mind as you lie there, trying to go to sleep.

Next morning

The next day Geordie remembered that old Scrimmie the caretaker used to keep a tranny in the room beside the boilerhouse. Nudge and Piff went to find it. They brought it back just in time to hear the news...

Radio news
...but the Prime Minister said that at this stage nothing more could be done... Arctic weather conditions still grip parts of Britain. In particular the area around Highton, which was struck by a freak blizzard yesterday is still under several feet of snow. Last night the temperature dropped to minus 15 degrees Centigrade and the weathermen say that there is no immediate chance of a thaw. So there is little hope yet of rescuing the schoolchildren marooned in the town's new comprehensive school. A council spokesman said that there has been no communication with the pupils and staff trapped inside the school, but that they should have been able to find enough supplies of food and clothing to keep them reasonably comfortable. Until the weather improves, he said, the children will just have to sit it out... In Bermuda today the famous American...

Thinking
1 It is impossible to get out of the school, but could you get a message out somehow? How could it be done? By signalling? Try to work out a method.
2 You are obviously going to be stuck in the school at least until tomorrow. What are you going to do with yourselves? How will you entertain yourselves?

Writing
1 Write a description of how you and some friends try to signal a message out of the school. Work out what the message is, who you want to send it to, and how you try to send it.
2 Make a detailed programme of activities and entertainments to cover the whole day.

Diversions . . .

Thinking　How many different games can you think of that would help to pass the time? They might be:

pencil and paper games
board games (you'd have to make the board and pieces)
ball games (you could use the gym or hall)
team games
acting games
card games (you might have to make the cards)

Writing　1　Make a list of all the indoor games you can think of.
2　Make up a board game or a pencil and paper game and explain the rules carefully.
or
Explain the rules of an indoor game that you already know.

. . . and alarms

A: I don't feel too good.
B: Why not?
A: It's my stomach. It feels as though it's on fire . . .

C: What's the matter with you?
D: Leave me alone.
C: What's wrong?
D: I just feel miserable.

Thinking　How might these snippets of conversation continue?

Writing　Choose one of the snippets and write out the whole conversation it comes from. Write in script. (See page 176)

Thaw!

Mary and Fizz went up on the roof. They came back very excited. It's started to thaw! Mr A went up to have a look for himself and it's true. He had a long talk with Miss B. After that he said he wanted five volunteers to help him dig a way out!

Thinking

1 Who will the five people be? Look at your class list and try to decide. *GRETA, JENNY, JOEL, SAN YUT, VIV.R.*

2 What should they take with them. Think of the useful tools and equipment that are in the school. Which would be most suitable for this journey? *FOOD, DRINK, FLASHLIGHTS, SHOVELS, WARM ARTICLES.*

Writing

MR. ~~DUGHES STEDDE~~

1 List the five people chosen. For each one write a short explanation of why he or she was chosen.

2 Make a list of the equipment they take with them.

3 Mr A is in charge of this team. Before they leave he has two conversations:

a with the five

b with Miss B

Write one of the conversations.

Letter home

Writing   Before the team leaves on its journey, everyone is allowed to write one letter home. These letters will be delivered if the team gets through all right. Write a letter to your family, telling them what has been happening, how you feel about it – and how you feel about being away from home.

The journey

Thinking   You are a member of the escape team. Look at the picture and imagine what it would be like to force your way through all that snow. Which route would you follow? Would you be successful?

Writing   Write the story of what happens on the journey – and whether it is successful or not.

Safe at last

STRANDED CHILDREN SAVED!

Thinking   Decide how it was that you were finally rescued.
Imagine that you are one of those interviewed by pressmen or TV reporters. What would you say about it all?

Writing   **1** Write the newspaper report that appeared after you had been rescued.

or

        2 Write the interview that you have with a TV reporter.
(Write in script – see page 176)

UNDERGROUND

This underground house was designed by the American architect Malcolm Wells. Similar houses have actually been built and used in Britain and the USA.

What would it be like to live in a house like this?

ENTRANCE

Designed in 1964, this first underground design of mine was never built, and yet it has been by far the most popular and widely published house I've ever designed.
I'd do it differently today, of course. There would be larger windows facing south and the insulation would be on the outside for greater thermal effeciency but I'd certainly try to keep the inviting, earthy freedom I stumbled upon here.

A RANDOM HOUSE

Manhunt underneath Vienna

Harry Lime was a criminal and black marketeer in Austria just after the Second World War. In this extract he has been hunted by the police and has taken refuge in the sewers beneath the city of Vienna.

What a strange world unknown to most of us lies under our feet. We live above a land of waterfalls and rushing rivers. Down there, tides ebb and flow as in the world above. This was such a place where Harry Lime made his last stand. The main sewer, which is half as wide as the Thames, rushes by under a huge arch. It is fed by streams which have fallen in waterfalls from higher levels. They are purified as they come down, so that the air is foul only in the side channels. The main stream smells sweet and fresh. Everywhere in the darkness is the sound of falling and rushing water. It was just past high tide when Martins and the policemen reached the river. First came the curving staircase, then a short passage so low they had to stoop. Then the shallow edge of the water lapped at their feet. My man (Bates) shone his torch along the edge of the torrent and said, 'He's gone that way.' The sewer left a scum of orange peel, old cigarette cartons and the like in the quiet water against the wall. Lime had left his trail in this scum as unmistakably as if he had walked in mud. My policeman shone his torch ahead with his left hand, and carried his gun in his right. He said to Martins, 'Keep behind me, sir, the swine may shoot.'

'Then why should you be in front?'

'It's my job, sir.' The water came halfway up their legs as they walked. Bates kept his torch pointing down and ahead at the trail at the sewer's edge. He said, 'The silly thing is that he doesn't stand a chance. The manholes are guarded and we've cordoned off the way into the Russian Zone. All our chaps have to do now is to sweep inwards down the side passages from the manholes.' He took a whistle out of his pocket and blew. Very far away, here and again there, came the notes of reply. He said, 'They are all down here now. The sewer police, I mean. They know this place as well as I know the Tottenham Court Road. I wish my old woman could see me now.'

He lifted his torch for a moment to shine it ahead. At that moment the shot came. The torch flew out of his hand and fell in the stream. Bates cried out. At the same moment a searchlight from fifty yards ahead lit the whole channel and caught Harry Lime in its beam. I could now also see Martins, and the staring eyes of Bates, who was slumped at the water's edge. The sewage washed to his waist. An empty cigarette carton wedged into his armpit and stayed. My party had reached the scene.

Martins stood dithering there above Bates' body, with Harry Lime halfway between us. We couldn't shoot for fear of hitting Martins. The light of the searchlight dazzled Lime. We moved slowly on, our revolvers trained for a chance. Lime turned this way and that like a rabbit dazzled by headlights. Then he suddenly took a flying jump into the deep central rushing stream. When we turned the searchlights after him he was submerged. The current of the sewer carried him rapidly on, past the body of Bates, out of the range of the searchlight into the dark. What makes a man without hope cling to a few more minutes of existence? Is it a good quality or a bad one? I have no idea.

Martins stood at the outer edge of the searchlight beam, staring downstream. He had his gun in his hand now. He was the only one of us who could fire with safety. I thought I saw a movement and called out to him, 'There. There. Shoot.' He lifted his gun and fired. A cry of pain came tearing back down the cavern.

Graham Greene, *The Third Man*

Questions to think and talk about	
1	Who was chasing Harry Lime?
2	How did they plan to catch him?
3	Who was Bates?
4	What happened to Bates?
5	What happened when they caught Lime in the beam of the searchlight?
6	Why did Lime not give himself up?

Writing

The manhunt described in this story took place many years ago. Write a description of a modern underground hunt. Here are some suggestions:

it might be a hunt for: a missing child
                       treasure
                       a hidden bomb
                       a criminal

it might take place: in the basement of a block of flats
                    in an underground carpark
                    in the London Underground
                    in a system of caves and potholes
                    in a deserted mine
                    in the cellars of a stately home or castle

Just a hole in the ground

Beneath the buildings and streets of a modern city exists the
network of walls, columns, cables, pipes, and tunnels required to
satisfy the basic needs of its inhabitants. The larger the city, the
more intricate this network becomes. While the walls and columns
5 support the city's buildings, bridges, and towers, the cables, pipes,
and tunnels carry life-sustaining elements such as water, electricity,
and gas. Larger tunnels burrow through the ground, linking places
on the congested surface more directly. Through them high-speed
trains carry the large numbers of people who live and work within
10 the urban community.

    Since this massive root system is rarely seen, even in part, its
complexity is difficult to imagine and its efficiency hardly ever
realized. Not until the underground breaks down or a water main
bursts do we begin to feel the extent of our dependence on this vast
15 hidden network.

    When a new street is being laid out, each utility is given a
specific location according to a master plan. The sewer and drains
are located farthest down and approximately under the centre of the
street. Closer both to the surface and to the sides of the street are the
20 water and gas pipes, while just 60 centimetres below the surface are
the electric and telephone cables.

    In an area requiring all these utilities, however, it is very rare
that a new street can conform completely to this ideal plan. Most
systems have grown gradually and randomly over many years and
25 since the problem is usually to increase or replace what already exists,
it is often necessary to squeeze things in wherever they will fit.

David Macauley, *Underground*

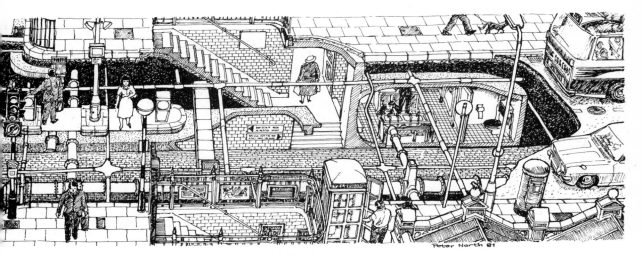

Questions

1 What are 'utilities'?

2 What are the main utilities that have to run beneath a city street?

3 Locate each of these on the drawing and write a sentence to explain where it is to be found: manhole, sewer, electricity supply, gas pipe, telephone cable.

4 Copy this diagram. Three pipes are not labelled. They are telephone, water, and sewer. Against each pipe write what you think it is. Lines 16–21 will help you do this.

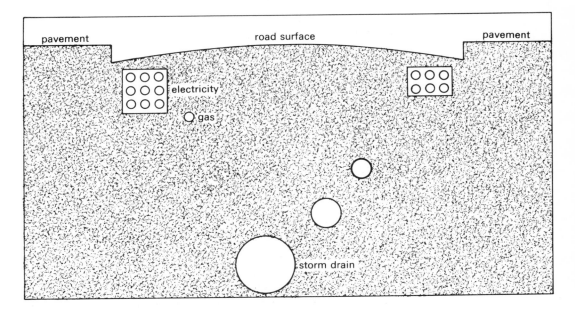

Escape from a prisoner-of-war camp

The tunnellers were dressed in woollen undervests and long pants, patched like harlequins, bright yellow from the puddled clay. On their heads they wore woollen caps or handkerchiefs knotted at the corners and, dancer-like, they wore no shoes.

Tyson, already in his tunnelling clothes, was waiting for them. 'Hurry up, chaps,' he said.

Peter and John quickly took off their outer clothing and joined the new shift, who were waiting to go below. It was cold and they shivered as Tyson slid under the boiler and, after much grunting and straining, disappeared from view. Peter, following, found a hole in the floor about two feet square. There was a rough ladder fixed to the side of the shaft, at the bottom of which the flickering rays of a lamp showed Tyson's legs as he crawled out of sight. Presently his face appeared where his legs had been. 'Go easy down the ladder,' he said.

At the bottom of the shaft was a square chamber about six feet by four in which a man crouched, working a crude concertina-like air pump made from a canvas kit-bag. By his side the goon lamp cast its lurid glow across his sweating face as he swung to the rhythm of the creaking pump. The walls and ceilings of the chamber and the mouth of the tunnel which opened from it were of solid wood, bed-boards jammed together side by side; but the floor was liquid clay.

Tyson was crouching half in and half out of the tunnel. In his hands he had two smoking lamps, one of which he passed to Peter. 'Follow me!' He spoke in a whisper, as though he could be heard through twelve feet of solid earth.

The tunnel, once they had left the chamber, was no longer lined with wood. The walls and ceiling dripped with water which gathered in long puddles on the floor and, as he wriggled after Tyson into the blackness, Peter felt this water soak through his woollen vest and the cold grip him with its icy fingers.

After crawling for about fifteen feet the light in front stopped moving, and when Peter caught up with it he found Tyson crouching over a hole in the tunnel floor, about three feet from where it came to an abrupt end. 'It goes down another six feet,' he whispered. 'The real tunnel starts from the bottom of this shaft. The upper tunnel is only a dummy. We camouflage the trapdoor over this shaft whenever we leave it, and then if the goons discover the upper tunnel they'll think it ends here. They'll just fill in the top shaft and this bit of tunnel – and then when the flap's all over we can strike the lower tunnel from another shaft. That way we only lose the short upper tunnel, and save the lower one.' He chuckled and climbed down the second ladder into the lower gallery.

Peter, stifling his feeling of panic, followed. This was what he had wanted. He'd got the chance, and now he must go through with it.

It seemed deep, deep down in the earth. Somehow the second shaft seemed a hundred times deeper than the first. It seemed completely beyond help from the surface. At intervals, where there had been a fall, patches of wooden shoring bulged ominously inwards. He had to fight hard to force himself to carry on.

He seemed to have been crawling for about half an hour before he again caught up with Tyson, who had reached the end of the tunnel. 'You work here,' Tyson told him. 'Here's a knife. Put the clay you dig out into this toboggan.' He showed Peter a rough wooden trough about eighteen inches long by twelve inches wide. 'When you pull the rope twice I'll haul it back to the lower shaft. I pass it up to the top tunnel, and John will send it back to the upper shaft in another toboggan. You see now why we need such a large team.'

When Tyson had left him there was silence; more complete silence than Peter had ever known. It seemed as though the eighteen feet of soil above his head was pressing down, pressing inwards. Then, in the silence, he heard the faint hiss of air pushed by the man at the pump through its life-line of jam tins joined end to end. This metal pipe, coming along the upper tunnel, down the shaft and along the wall of the lower tunnel, was his connexion with the outside world – that, and the rope which pulled the toboggan. He took the knife and began to hack away at the clay in front of him.

An hour later Tyson called a halt. John took Peter's place at the head of the tunnel, while Peter pulled the clay back to the lower shaft. The rope, thinly plaited from the sisal string off the Red Cross parcels, cut deeply into his hands, and the strain of pulling the heavy toboggan through the thick sludge of the tunnel floor made his shoulders ache. He had blisters on the palms of his hands from the handle of the knife and, as he unloaded the clay into jam tins and passed them up to Tyson at the top of the shaft, he began to realize that there was more to tunnelling than he had thought.

At the end of the two-hour shift they came to the surface. Peter now knew why the earlier tunnellers had staggered as they crossed the kitchen floor. He had been sweating for the last two hours, and his woollen underclothes were wringing wet with sweat and moisture from the tunnel.

Eric Williams, *The Tunnel*

Coal miner

The work of pick-and-shovel seems painfully simple at first. But think of the many movements the coal-face man must go through. All of them need great skill. Picture a man on his knees, hacking away at a wall of coal. Another man bent double is shovelling away what the first man breaks down. That's the scene. To be a coal-face worker all you need is a strong back, and be able or uncaring enough to take the sheer misery of conditions down there. The more I watch, though, the more I can see that a *real* collier needs a lot of intelligence and skill. For one thing, he must plan his own work. Most workers in industry have their work planned for them. The miner plans his own. He and he alone is the final judge of how a particular wall shall be attacked. He is the designer and the organizer and the doer. He must be, for he has to keep the flow of coal coming. He must also keep control of his own moods, and pay constant attention to the way the coal-wall is built. He must pay attention to all this, for there is the safety of his mates and himself to care for too.

It is no straightforward thing to use a pick-axe either. It takes a special skill to use it so as to bring down a wall of coal four feet six inches high by eight yards long. He must bring it down in such a way that the coal is broken into the correct and most useful sizes of chunks. These chunks weigh seventeen tons on average. They must come out safely, and yet not hold up production. Very often the collier has to make up for mistakes made by men on the previous shift. And the shifts are seven hours long or more every day. And the shifts keep changing, so he can never plan his life too well. It takes a great staying power to be a miner. In the end, you see, the collier at the face is responsible for his quota. The quota, or set amount of coal brought out, must be kept up. No excuses will do.

You do not see all this at once. I watched for a whole day before it began to dawn on me. What did strike me first was this willingness to work incredibly hard, and the need for teamwork, endurance, and co-operation. If you don't have these, you are done for. If the gaffer or foreman does not find you out, your mates will. Your work-mates will then have to carry you, but that will not last for long. They see to that.

Clancy Sigal, *Weekend in Dinlock*

A Collier's Wife

Somebody's knocking at the door
    Mother, come down and see.
– I's think it's nobbut a beggar,
    Say, I'm busy.

It's not a beggar, mother, – hark
    How hard he knocks . . .
– Eh, tha'rt a mard-'arsed kid,
    'E'll gi'e thee socks!

Shout an' ax what 'e wants,
    I canna come down.
– 'E says 'Is it Arthur Holliday's?'
    Say 'Yes,' tha clown.

'E says, 'Tell your mother as 'er mester's
    Got hurt i' th' pit.'
What – oh my sirs, 'e never says that,
    That's niver it.

Come out o' the way an' let me see,
    Eh, there's no peace!
An' stop thy scraightin' childt,
    Do shut thy face.

[handwritten: m]

[handwritten: I think it's just a begger, tell him I'm busy]

'Your mester's had an accident,
    An' they're ta'en 'im i' th' ambulance
To Nottingham,' – Eh dear o' me
    If 'e's not a man for mischance!

Wheers he hurt this time, lad?
    – I dunna know,
They on'y towd me it wor bad –
    It would be so!

Eh, what a man! an' that cobbly road,
    They'll jolt him a'most to death,
I'm sure he's in for some trouble
    Nigh every time he takes breath.

Out o' my way, childt – dear o' me, wheer
    Have I put his clean stockings and shirt;
Goodness knows if they'll be able
    To take off his pit dirt.

An' what moan he'll make – there niver
    Was such a man for a fuss
If anything ailed him – at any rate
    I shan't have him to nuss.

I do hope it's not very bad!
    Eh, what a shame it seems
As some should ha'e hardly a smite o' trouble
    An' others has reams.

It's a shame as 'e should be knocked about
    Like this, I'm sure it is!
He's had twenty accidents, if he's had one;
    Owt bad, an' it's his.

There's one thing, we'll have peace for a bit,
    Thank heaven for a peaceful house;
An' there's compensation, sin' it's accident,
    An' club money – ' nedn't grouse.

An' a fork an' a spoon he'll want, an' what else;
    I s'll never catch that train –
What a traipse it is if a man gets hurt –
    I s'd think he'll get right again.

D. H. Lawrence

Orpheus and Eurydice

This Greek myth tells of the love of the musician Orpheus for his young and beautiful wife Eurydice. Orpheus played the lyre more beautifully than anyone in the world. Not long after Orpheus and Eurydice were married, Eurydice was bitten on the foot by a viper and died.

In despair Orpheus went to seek his lost wife in the regions of the dead. He went down into the underworld by a steep and narrow way which began in a gloomy cave. Down and down the path wound until it reached the grey and dreary realm of Hades. Passing through crowds of ghosts, Orpheus made his way towards the throne of the king and queen. At the sight of the wild-eyed musician with his lyre, the god Hades raised his hand for silence and bade the stranger play. With his right hand Orpheus struck the lyre and, lifting his voice, began to plead and mourn in tones which moved the hardest hearts and brought tears to the eyes of many.

'O god and goddess,' sang Orpheus, 'to whom we must all come at last, listen, I pray, to my tale, for I speak the truth. I am come to plead for your mercy and to beg you to give back life to my beloved Eurydice, who was slain by the cruel viper when our wedding rites were scarcely over. Give her back to me, I beg, for she has done no harm and broken no vow. Gods of the underworld, we shall all come under your rule in time, but until she has lived her proper span, give her back to me, I implore you.'

So piteously did Orpheus lament, with such skill did he draw harmony from the strings that the inhabitants of Hades came from near and far to hear his music. The ghosts came in crowds, like flocks of birds coming home to roost at dusk, or like showers of dead leaves driven by the autumn wind. There were boys and men, unmarried girls, the spirits of great heroes and of nameless ones who had died in battle on land or sea. All who heard were touched to the heart by the music of Orpheus; all pitied the young man.

Among those who heard Orpheus were the prisoners in Hades, doomed to suffer eternal punishment for their crimes on earth. Tantalus was one. He was condemned to lie beneath a tree at the edge of a pool. Every time he stretched out his hand to gather fruit, a wind blew the branches out of reach. Every time he approached the pool to quench his thirst, the water drew back. Another was Ixion, whose punishment was to be tied to a wheel which turned for ever. When Orpheus sang, the wheel stood still, and Ixion was for a while relieved of his torment. Sisyphus, for his crimes on earth, was condemned to roll a heavy stone up a hill; as soon as it reached the top, it rolled down again, so that his labour was eternal. For the first time he was allowed to rest upon his stone half-way up the hill, while Orpheus lamented. For the first time, too, the cheeks of the Furies were wet with tears. These were among the most terrible deities in Hades – three-winged women whose purpose was to avenge crimes such as the killing of a parent or a child. Some say that their look was made fiercer by writhing serpents which crowned their heads, like the serpents of the gorgon Medusa. Now even the snakes ceased their writhing and hissing to listen to Orpheus.

By the time the song was finished, Persephone, queen of the underworld, could not restrain her pity, and she looked at her husband and pleaded for the life of Eurydice. Hades, stern king, consented, and the young bride was summoned from among the newly arrived ghosts. Limping upon her wounded foot, Eurydice appeared, pale and beautiful, before the throne. Long and lovingly Orpheus looked at her, but he dared not approach until the king had given his judgement. Because of his steadfastness in love, said the king, Orpheus would be allowed to take her back to the earth on one condition: he was to lead the way, and Eurydice would follow. He must not look back at her, even for an instant, until they reached the upper air. If he did, he would lose her once more – this time for ever.

Eagerly Orpheus embraced his wife. Then, taking leave of the king and queen, they began the journey back to earth. Orpheus went in front, Eurydice behind, as they had been bidden. Once the gloomy regions of ghosts were passed, they came to a place of terrible darkness and silence, groping their way between rocks and through dark passages where icy water dripped about them, and jagged rocks tore their clothes. Then they began to climb, up and up along the winding track by which Orpheus had come. Panting, he reached a sort of ledge or platform not far from where the track led into the cave where it would end in the light of day. Suddenly a madness overcame Orpheus. A terrible fear for his beloved Eurydice made him forget his promise to the king of the underworld. He looked back to see if he could make our her form in the darkness behind him, and in that instant she was lost to him.

A great roll of thunder came from the underworld. Amidst the thunder Orpheus heard the voice of Eurydice:

'O Orpheus, the Fates are calling me back. Unseen hands are dragging me down. I feel faint, and I no longer have any power to resist.'

In vain did Orpheus stretch out his arms to embrace her. She floated like a cloud of grey smoke back into the depths of Hades. He had lost her for ever.

James Reeves, *Islands and Palaces*

Puzzles

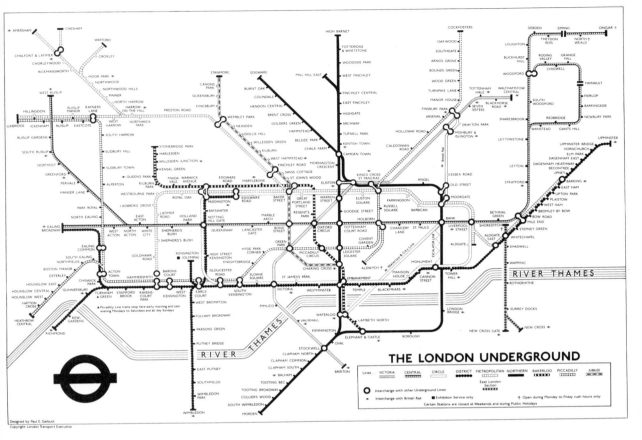

1   What is the shortest route between these stations:
   a   Liverpool Street and Victoria
   b   Paddington and Elephant and Castle
   c   Ealing Broadway and Arnos Grove
   d   London Bridge and Bethnal Green
   e   Clapham Common and Edgware Road?

Note: by shortest route we mean the route that has the least number of stations on it.

2   What is the least number of times you would have to change trains to travel between these stations:
   a   Pimlico and Regents Park
   b   Holloway Road and West Hampstead
   c   Maida Vale and Green Park
   d   Hornchurch and Goodge Street
   e   Southgate and Shadwell?

Word study

All these words occur in this unit. The number after each one tells you the page it is on.

scum   56
torrent   56
congested   58
ominously   61
rites   65
steadfastness   66

1 Find each word and read the sentence it is in.
2 Write each word on a new line, and against it, write what you think it means. If you are not sure, try to work out what it means from the sentence.
3 Look *all* the words up in the dictionary.
4 Write the correct meanings of any that you got wrong.

POSSIBLE FUTURES

Here are two artists' impressions of the future.
Do you agree with their views?

Martians

I could hear a number of noises, almost like those of an engine-shed, and the place rocked with that beating thud. Through the aperture in the wall I could see the top of a tree touched with gold, and the warm blue of a tranquil evening sky. For a minute or so I remained watching the curate, who was trapped with me, and then I advanced, crouching and stepping with extreme care amidst the broken crockery that littered the floor.

I touched the curate's leg, and he started so violently that a mass of plaster went sliding down outside and fell with a loud impact. I gripped his arm, fearing he might cry out, and for a long time we remained motionless. Then I turned to see how much of our rampart remained. By raising myself cautiously across a beam I was able to see out of this gap into what had been overnight a quiet suburban roadway. Vast indeed was the change that we beheld.

The fifth travel-cylinder must have fallen right into the midst of a house we had first visited. The building had vanished, completely smashed, pulverized and dispersed by the blow. The cylinder lay now far beneath the original foundations, deep in a hole, already vastly larger than the pit I had looked into at Woking. The earth all round it had splashed under that tremendous impact – 'splashed' is the only word – and lay in heaped piles that hid the masses of the adjacent houses. Our house had collapsed backwards. We hung now

on the very verge of the great circular pit the Martians were engaged in making.

They were, I now saw, the most unearthly creatures it is possible to conceive. They were huge round bodies – or, rather, heads – about four feet in diameter, each body having in front of it a face. This face had no nostrils, but it had a pair of very large, dark-coloured eyes, and just beneath this a kind of fleshy beak. In the back of this head or body – I scarcely know how to speak of it – was the single tight tympanic surface, since known to be anatomically an ear, though it must have been almost useless, in our denser air. In a group round the mouth were sixteen slender, almost whip-like tentacles, arranged in two bunches of eight each. These bunches have since been named rather aptly, the *hands*. For the first time in my sight they seemed to be endeavouring to raise themselves on these hands, but of course, with the increased weight of terrestrial conditions, this was impossible.

. . . I crouched, watching a Fighting Machine closely. And suddenly I heard a yell, and saw a long tentacle reaching over the shoulder of the machine to the little cage that hunched upon its back. Then something – something struggling violently – was lifted high against the sky, and as this black object came down again, I saw by the green brightness of their work-smoke that it was a man. For an instant he was clearly visible. He was a stout, ruddy, middle-aged man, well-dressed; three days before he must have been walking the world, a man of considerable consequence. I could see his staring eyes and gleams of light on his studs and watch-chain. He vanished behind a mound, and for a moment there was silence. And then began a shrieking and a sustained and cheerful hooting from the Martians . . .

H. G. Wells, *The War of the Worlds* (1898)

Questions to think and talk about

1 What has happened before this extract begins? *the martians attacked*
2 What do the Martians look like? *huge round heads approx 4 feet diameter*
3 What is their attitude towards human beings? *enemies*
4 Suppose this was really happening *now*: what could human beings do about the Martians? *Kill them*
5 Who would win?

each body having a face in front of it. No nostrils. large dark eyes fleshy

Writing

1 It is the day after the first landing of the Martians.
The Daily Gazette comes out with this front page headline:
MARTIAN TERROR IN SURREY
Write the report that follows it.

2 The Government is fighting the Martians. You are Prime Minister. Describe how you plan the campaign against them and what happens in the end.

Space colonies

In 1975 the American space scientists of NASA prepared a plan for the first space colony. They designed a space station where a large number of people could live and work permanently in space. They say that all the knowledge and skills needed to build such a station already exist.

5

The colony they designed is like a wheel a mile across. The rim of the wheel is a huge tube in which the people live and work. It is connected by six spokes to a central hub. This is where spaceships arrive and depart.

10

There is no gravity in space and this makes life difficult for people who are used to living on earth. This problem is overcome by making the colony spin like a top. It is lit by natural sunshine. Part of the wheel is used for farming. Although the colony has a population of 10,000 the use of modern farming methods means that they can all be fed from only 150 acres. All the power needs are supplied by solar energy.

15

All the people have to work for their living, of course. Some of

them are mineralogists, travelling to and from the moon by rocket.
On the moon there are mines from which they extract various
20 minerals. On the colony itself factories manufacture small space
power stations. These are satellites which collect solar energy and
transmit it to the earth. Other factories manufacture parts for new
colonies elsewhere in space.

Other American scientists have studied the possibility of
25 travelling to the stars. The problem is that the distances involved are
vast. The nearest stars are two light years away. Light travels at
186,000 miles per *second* (or over 66 million miles an hour.) When
you consider that there are nearly 9,000 hours in a year, you begin to
realize just how far away even the nearest stars are.

30 One scientist has worked out a scheme to travel to the stars. He
suggests a huge spaceship propelled by nuclear power. The ship is
like a travelling colony: it has to be, since the journey takes hundreds
of years. On board live people, animals, and plants. Of course,
those who begin the journey die before it is even a quarter over. It is
35 their great-great-great-great-great-grandchildren who eventually
arrive at the stars!

Questions

1 Draw a plan of the space colony and show on it:
  a where the people live
  b where the spaceships arrive.
2 How many people will live in the space colony? 10,000
3 How much space is used on the colony for farming? 150 acres
4 Where does the colony get its electricity from? Solar energy
5 What work do the people who live on the colony do, apart from
farming and mining? manufacturing
6 What is the greatest problem in travelling to the stars? the distances are vast.
7 How would the spaceship be powered? nuclear power

True or false?

1 Men already have the technology to build a space colony. T
2 The colony spins like a top to provide energy. F
3 The colony cannot provide all its own food. F
4 Some of the people on the colony would have to travel to the moon
to work. T
5 It would take centuries to travel to the nearest star. T
6 The people who reached the stars would be children. T

Writing

You are a member of a family travelling to the stars.

a Describe a typical day on board the star ship.
b You have just been told about the facts of the journey. The
spaceship will not reach the stars for another 235 years. You and your
parents will be dead long before then. Describe how you feel when
you learn this.

Bleep

Bleep! said the little robot spacecraft,
squatting infinitely alone
in the blinding dust of Venus,
bleep . . . bleep . . . bleep – Bleep
Fifty-million miles of empty space
were crossed in seconds –
mankind knew of contact
with the sky's love goddess at last –
and earphones jabbered at Jodrell Bank.

But nothing could be made there
of such strange noises
(for the bleeps were in Russian, you see);
only the Russian scientists, somewhere in
Siberia,
knew what such noises meant . . .

And the bleeps said: 'By God! By Comrade
Khrushchev –
it's bloody hot here! It's far too hot
for a little Russian rocket like me – I'm
getting out of here!'

'Nonsense,' replied the scientists,
somewhere in Siberia, 'you can't *feel*
anything, you're only a robot,
and you just can't get out, so there!'
(But, secretly, they worried about
radiation and mutation,
computerized constipation,
and galactic goo gumming up the works.)

'Like hell I can't get out,'
snarled the little rocket,
'just you watch my space-dust!'
and he took off for Alpha Centauri
at a most remarkable speed.

'Amazing!' cried the scientists,
as the dot on the telescope dwindled
out into the dark infinity.

Bleep, said the little spacecraft,
nipping smartly past Neptune,
bleep . . . bleep . . . bleep . . . bleep . . .

Bryn Griffiths

The First Men on Mercury

– We come in peace from the third planet.
Would you take us to your leader?

    – Bawr stretter! Bawr. Bawr. Stretterhawl?

– This is a little plastic model
of the solar system, with working parts.
You are here and we are there and we
are now here with you, is this clear?

    – Gawl horrop. Bawr. Abawrhannahanna!

– Where we come from is blue and white
with brown, you see we call the brown
here 'land', the blue is 'sea', and the white
is 'clouds' over land and sea, we live
on the surface of the brown land,
all round is sea and clouds. We are 'men'.
Men come –

    – Glawp men! Gawrbenner menko. Menhawl?

– Men come in peace from the third planet
which we call 'earth'. We are earthmen.
Take us earthmen to your leader.

    – Thmen? Thmen? Bawr. Bawrhossop.
    Yuleeda tan hanna. Harrabost yuleeda.

– I am the yuleeda. You see my hands,
we carry no benner, we come in peace.
The spaceways are all stretterhawn.

    – Glawn peacemen all horrabhanna tantko!
    Tan come at'mstrossop. Glawp yuleeda!

– Atoms are peacegawl in our harraban.
Menbat worrabost from tan hannahanna.

    – You men we know bawrhossoptant. Bawr.
    We know yuleeda. Go strawg backspetter quick.

– We cantantabawr, tantingko
backspetter now!

    – Banghapper now! Yes, third planet back.
    Yuleeda will go back blue, white, brown
    nowhanna! There is no more talk.

– Gawl han fasthapper?

    – No. You must go back to your planet.
    Go back in peace, take what you have gained
    but quickly.

– Stretterworra gawl, gawl . . .

    – Of course, but nothing is ever the same,
    now is it? You'll remember Mercury.

Edwin Morgan

QT-1

Powell felt a sudden sympathy for the robot. It was not like the ordinary robot which did the single job it was designed to do. This one, QT-1, known as 'Cutie', was different. He placed a hand on Cutie's shoulder. The metal was cold and hard to the touch.

'Cutie,' he said, 'I'm going to try to explain something to you. You are the first robot who has ever asked *why* he exists. I think your special intelligence will allow you to understand.'

The Earthman opened a square window looking into space. The strong, clear glass revealed deep space, thick with stars.

'What do you think that is?' asked Powell.

'Exactly what it seems,' replied Cutie. 'A black material just beyond the glass, and it is spotted with little gleaming dots.'

'Now listen carefully. The blackness you see is emptiness. Vast emptiness stretching out infinitely. The little gleaming dots are huge masses of energy-filled matter. We call them stars. Some of them are millions of miles in diameter. This space station is only one mile in diameter. The dots seem tiny because they are so far off. Some of these dots are not stars, but what we call planets. Worlds that human beings live on. The one you see right in the bottom right-hand corner of the window is our own planet. Good old Earth. Three billions of human beings live there, Cutie.'

The red glow of Cutie's electronic eyes looked at Powell. 'Do you,' said Cutie slowly, 'expect me to believe any such complicated, unlikely tale as you have just told me? What do you take me for? Globes of energy millions of miles across! Worlds with three billions of humans on them! Infinite emptiness! A dot is a dot.' He paused. 'Look at you. The material you are made of is soft and flabby. It lacks endurance and strength. You depend for energy on the wasteful consumption of vegetable and meaty stuff – like *that*!' He pointed a disapproving finger at the remains of Donovan's sandwich. 'You pass regularly into a coma you call sleep. The least change in humidity or temperature interferes with your abilities. You are *makeshift*!'

He rose erect. 'On the other hand, I am perfectly made. I absorb energy directly and I use it without wastage. I am made of strong metal. I am continuously awake, and can stand extremes of conditions quite easily. It is obvious, you'll agree, that no being can create another being that is superior to the maker. So your silly explanation is nothing!'

Isaac Asimov, *I, Robot*

An ape about the house

Granny thought it a perfectly horrible idea; but then, she could remember the days when there were *human* servants.

'If you imagine,' she snorted, 'that I'll share the house with a monkey, you're very much mistaken.'

'Don't be so old-fashioned,' I answered. 'Anyway, Dorcas isn't a monkey.'

'Then what is she – it?'

I flipped through the pages of the Biological Engineering Corporation's guide. 'Listen to this, Gran, I said. ' "The Superchimp (Registered Trade-mark) *Pan Sapiens* is an intelligent anthropoid, derived by selective breeding and genetic modification from basic chimpanzee stock –" '

'Just what I said! A monkey!'

' " – and with a large-enough vocabulary to understand simple orders. It can be trained to perform all types of domestic work or routine manual labour and is docile, affectionate, housebroken, and particularly good with children – " '

'Children! Would you trust Johnnie and Susan with a – a *gorilla*?'

I put the handbook down with a sigh.

'You've got a point there. Dorcas *is* expensive, and if I find the little monsters knocking her about –'

At this moment, fortunately the door buzzer sounded. 'Sign, please,' said the delivery man. I signed, and Dorcas entered our lives.

'Hello, Dorcas,' I said. 'I hope you'll be happy here.'

Her big, mournful eyes peered out at me from beneath their heavy ridges. I'd met much uglier humans, though she was rather an odd shape, being only about four feet tall and very nearly as wide. In her neat, plain uniform she looked just like a maid from one of those early twentieth-century movies; her feet, however, were bare and covered an astonishing amount of floor space.

'Morning Ma'am,' she answered, in slurred but perfectly intelligible accents.

'She can speak!' squawked Granny.

'Of course,' I answered. 'She can pronounce over fifty words, and can understand two hundred.'

Arthur C. Clarke

THEN	NOW	NEXT

  ?

  ?

 ?

Puzzles

More about Dorcas

The story *An ape about the house* continues like this:

1 One of Granny's cigarettes finally did the trick.
2 Dorcas settled down very quickly.
3 It took several weeks before I discovered her limitations and allowed for them; at first it was quite hard to remember that she was not exactly human, and that it was no good engaging her in the sort of conversations we women occupy ourselves with when we get together.
4 At first she had an annoying habit of picking up things with her feet; it seemed as natural to her as using her hands, and it took a long time to break her of it.
5 She was good-natured, conscientious, and didn't answer back. Of course, she was not terribly bright, and some jobs had to be explained to her at great length before she got the point.
6 Her basic training – Class A Domestic, plus Nursery Duties – had been excellent, and by the end of the first month there were very few jobs around the house that she couldn't do, from laying the table to changing the children's clothes.
7 Or not many of them; she did have an interest in clothes, and was fascinated by colours.

Clearly these sentences are in the wrong order. Read them through and write down the numbers of the sentences in the correct order.

Word study

All these words occur in this unit. The number after each one tells you the page it is on.

colony   72
transmit   73
eventually   73
dwindled   74

revealed   76
makeshift   76
vocabulary   77
routine   77

1   Find each word and read the sentence it is in.
2   Write each word on a new line, and against it write what you think it means.
3   When you have done all eight, look them *all* up in the dictionary.
4   Write the correct meanings of any that you got wrong.

The solar system

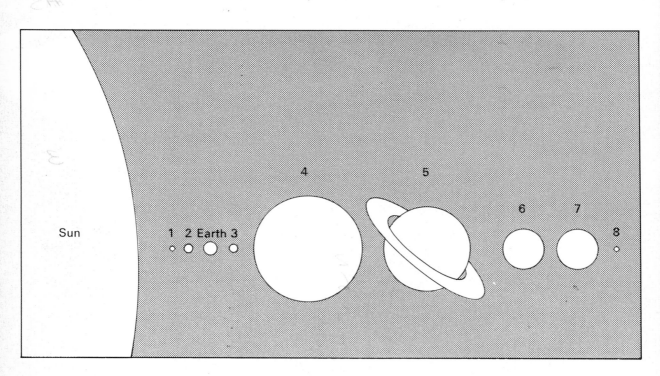

Can you name the planets in the solar system? Match the correct letter to each number.

A   Mars
B   Saturn
C   Pluto
D   Mercury

E   Neptune
F   Jupiter
G   Venus
H   Uranus

THE HORROR...
THE **HORROR!**

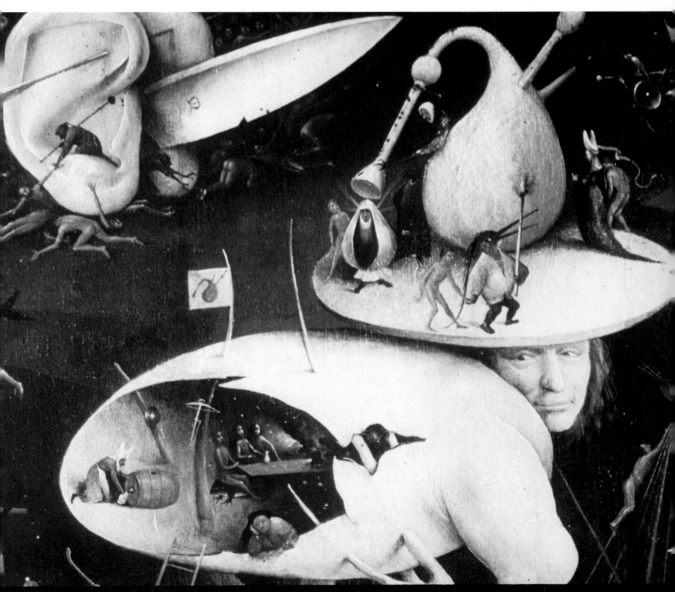

Detail from *The Garden of Earthly Delights* by **Hieronymous Bosch** (Prado, Madrid).

This is a painting by a medieval artist, showing the most horrible things he could imagine.
Do you find them horrible?
What has he done to make the creatures and the actions frightening?
Some people would say this picture is 'nightmare-ish'. What is a

Terror in the night

It is Christmas time. Carrie and Nick have been sent across country to an isolated cottage where a woman called Hepzibah lives, to collect a Christmas goose; but they have been told frightening stories about this place.

It was growing dusk; stars were pricking out in the cold sky above them. And it was so quiet, suddenly, that their ears seemed to be singing.

Carrie whispered, 'There's the path down. By that stone.'

Nick's pale face glimmered as he looked up at her. He whispered back, 'You go. I'll wait here.'

'Don't be silly.' Carrie swallowed – then pleaded with him. 'Don't you want a nice mince pie? We might get a mince pie. And it's not far.'

Nick shook his head. He screwed up his eyes and put his hands over his ears.

Carrie said coldly, 'All right, have it your own way. But it'll be dark soon and you'll be really scared then. Much more scared by yourself than you would be with me.

And she marched off without looking back.

She hadn't gone far when she heard Nick wailing behind her, 'Carrie, wait for me, *wait* . . .' She stopped and he skidded into her back. 'Don't leave me, Carrie!'

'I thought it was you leaving *me*,' she said, making a joke of it, to comfort him, and he tried to laugh but it turned into a sob in his throat.

He hung on to the back of her coat, whimpering under his breath as she led the way down the path. The yew trees grew densely, some of them covered with ivy that rustled and rattled. Like scales, Carrie thought; the trees were like live creatures with scales. She told herself not to be stupid, but stopped to draw breath. She said, 'Do be quiet, Nick.'

'Why?'

'I don't know,' Carrie said. 'Something . . .'

She couldn't explain it. It was such a strange feeling. As if there was something here, something *waiting*. Deep in the trees or deep in the earth. Something old and huge and nameless, Carrie thought, and started to tremble. Then she heard it. A kind of slow, dry whisper, or sigh. As if the earth were turning in its sleep. Or the huge, nameless thing were breathing.

'Did you hear?' Carrie said. 'Did you *hear*?'

Nick began to cry piteously. Silence now, except for his weeping.

Carrie said, dry-mouthed, 'It's gone now. It wasn't anything. There's nothing there, really.'

Nick gulped, trying hard to stop crying. Then he clutched Carrie. 'Yes there is! There is *now*!'

Carrie listened. It wasn't the sound she had heard before but something quite different. A queer, throaty, chuckling, gobbling sound that seemed to come from somewhere above them, higher up the path. They stood still as stone. The sound was coming closer.

'*Run*,' Carrie said. She begun to run, stumbling. The big bag they had brought for the goose caught between her legs and almost threw her down but she recovered her balance, her feet slipping and sliding. She ran, and Nick ran behind her, and the creature, whatever it was, the gobbling *Thing*, followed them. It seemed to be calling to them and Carrie thought of fairy tales she had read – you looked back at something behind you and were caught in its spell! She gasped, 'Don't look back, Nick, whatever you do.'

The path widened and flattened as it came out of the Grove and she caught Nick's hand to make him run faster. Too fast for his shorter legs and he fell on his knees. He moaned, as she pulled him up, 'I can't, I *can't* Carrie . . .'

'Yes you *can*. Not much farther.'

They saw the house then, its dark, tall-chimneyed bulk looming up, and lights in the windows. One light quite high up and one low down, at the side. They ran, on rubbery legs, through an open gate and across a dirt yard towards the lit window. There was a door but it was shut. They flung themselves against it.

Gobble-Gobble was behind them, was crossing the yard.

'Please,' Carrie croaked. 'Please.' Quite sure that it was too late, that the creature would get them.

Nina Bawden, *Carrie's War*

<table>
<tr><td>Questions to think
and talk about</td><td>1</td><td>What was the place they were walking through like?</td></tr>
<tr><td></td><td>2</td><td>How old do you think they were?</td></tr>
<tr><td></td><td>3</td><td>What is the difference between the way each behaves?</td></tr>
<tr><td></td><td>4</td><td>What do you think Gobble-Gobble is?</td></tr>
<tr><td></td><td>5</td><td>Many people enjoy watching horror films or reading frightening books. Why do you think this is?</td></tr>
<tr><td></td><td>6</td><td>What is the most frightening thing that you have seen or read about?</td></tr>
</table>

Writing   Write about a real experience, or make up a story, with the title, Terror in the Night.

The Amityville horror

The Lutz family moved to New York in 1975. There were five of them: Kathleen and George, and their three children, Danny, Chris, and Missy. They had looked at almost fifty houses before deciding at first sight that 112 Ocean Avenue, Amityville was just what they wanted. On December 18th they moved in.

Twenty-eight days later the Lutz family fled from the house in the middle of the night. They claimed that their lives had been tormented by ghosts, horrible smells, and blood-chilling screams. The furniture had moved all by itself and green slime had oozed from the floor and walls. They had even seen a snorting, horrifically-ugly, red-eyed pig.

George Lutz felt that the evil spirits had been passed on to them from the last owners of the house, the De Feo Family. In the middle of the night of November 13th 1974, Ronald De Feo went mad with a gun and several people were killed. At his trial he said, 'I heard voices. Whenever I looked round there was no one there . . . It just started. It went too fast. I couldn't stop.'

Later the Lutz family said that they had found out that the land on which the house was built had been used by the Indians for centuries as a centre for devil-worship. Many people, however, laughed at the story and said that George Lutz had used his imagination to make a fortune. They said that he had known about the De Feo murders all the time. He was using Ronald De Feo's madness to make himself wealthy by inventing stories about various terrifying events. Fleeing from the house in the middle of the night was just part of the hoax.

George Lutz did make money from his experiences. A book was written about what the family claimed to have seen and heard. It sold more than four million copies. The film of the book was released in the United States in July 1979, and within six months it had earned £30 million. The film makers used a different house which looked just like 112 Ocean Avenue, because they were unwilling to use the house itself. The producer said, 'Where would we be if someone was hurt there because of the presence of strange forces?'

Many thousands of Americans believed the story of the Lutz family. The house became a tourist attraction; a seemingly endless stream of people wanted to see or hear for themselves the ghoulish sights and sounds said to be there. The new owners of the house were critical of the Lutz family and said that they did not believe their tales of terror. Nevertheless the sight-seers continued to come; the book continued to sell; and the film went on making money.

Questions

1 What house did Mr and Mrs Lutz buy?
2 How long did they live in it?
3 Why did they leave it so suddenly?
4 What had happened there about a year before?
5 Why did George Lutz say that this had affected his family?
6 What had the place been used for in the past?
7 Why did some people not believe the Lutzs' story?
8 What did George Lutz do after leaving the house?
9 Why was 112 Ocean Avenue not used for the film?
10 What did the Lutz family really see at 112 Ocean Avenue?

Writing: your opinion, please

1 Do you think the Lutz family were telling the truth? What are the reasons for your opinion?
2 Does it matter if they were telling the truth or not, so long as it makes a good story? Why?
3 If you were given the chance, would you visit a house like 112 Ocean Avenue? Would you stay the night? Explain why.
4 Why do so many people read horror books and go to see horror films?

The thing

Slowly, shakily, with unnatural and inhuman movements a human form, scarlet in the firelight, crawled out on to the floor of the cave. It was the Un-man, of course: dragging its broken leg and with its lower jaw sagging open like that of a corpse, it raised itself to a standing position. And then, close behind it, something else came up out of the hole. First came what looked like branches of trees, and then seven or eight spots of light, irregularly grouped like a constellation. Then a tubular mass which reflected the red glow as if it were polished. His heart gave a great leap as the branches suddenly resolved themselves into long wiry feelers and the dotted lights became the many eyes of a shell-helmeted head and the mass that followed it was revealed as a large roughly cylindrical body. Horrible things followed – angular, many jointed legs, and presently, when he thought the whole body was in sight, a second body came following it and after that a third. The thing was in three parts, united only by a kind of wasp's waist structure – three parts that did not seem to be truly aligned and made it look as if it had been trodden on – a huge, many-legged, quivering deformity, standing just behind the Un-man so that the horrible shadows of both danced in enormous and united menace on the wall of rock behind them.

C. S. Lewis, *Perelandra*

Prince Kano

In a dark wood Prince Kano lost his way
And searched in vain through the long summer's day.
At last, when night was near, he came in sight
Of a small clearing filled with yellow light,
And there, bending beside his brazier, stood
A charcoal burner wearing a black hood.
The Prince cried out for joy: 'Good friend, I'll give
What you will ask: guide me to where I live.'
The man pulled back his hood: he had no face –
Where it should be there was an empty space.
Half dead with fear the Prince staggered away,
Rushed blindly through the wood till break of day;
And then he saw a larger clearing, filled
With houses, people; but his soul was chilled,
He looked around for comfort, and his search
Led him inside a small, half-empty church

Where monks prayed. 'Father,' to one he said,
'I've seen a dreadful thing; I am afraid.'
'What did you see, my son?' 'I saw a man
Whose face was like . . .' and, as the Prince began,
The monk drew back his hood and seemed to hiss,
Pointing to where his face should be, 'Like this?'

Edward Lowbury

A Meeting

When George began to climb all unawares
He saw a horrible face at the top of the stairs.

The rats came tumbling down the planks,
Pushing past without a word of thanks.

The rats were thin, the stairs were tall,
But the face at the top was the worst of all.

It wasn't the ghost of his father or mother.
When they are laid there's always another.

It wasn't the ghost of people he knew.
It was worse than this, shall I tell you who?

It was himself, oh what a disgrace.
And soon they were standing face to face.

At first they pretended neither cared
But when they met they stood and stared.

One started to smile and the other to frown,
And one moved up and the other moved down.

But which emerged and which one stays,
Nobody will know till the end of his days.

George D. Painter

A guide to horrorland

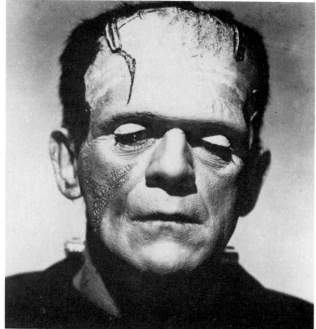

DRACULA

This famous character from horror films and fiction first made his appearance in a novel by Bram Stoker. The story is told by an English gentleman who travels to the area of central Europe known as Transylvania. There he meets the strange and terrifying Count Dracula. Transylvania is a region particularly noted for its werewolves and vampires. It soon becomes clear that the Count is indeed a vampire. During the daytime he is a corpse, but at night he comes to life as a charming and civilized man . . . until his victim comes near. He is pursuing a beautiful heroine, who manages to escape his clutches. At last she is able to overcome the monster and drive a stake through his wicked heart, thus ridding the world of him for ever.

FRANKENSTEIN

Together with Dracula, Frankenstein is the most famous of horror film characters. The central character is not Frankenstein at all, but a hideous monster built up from parts of human corpses. The original story was told by Mary Shelley and was entitled *Frankenstein, or the Modern Prometheus*. In this novel, published in 1818, Frankenstein was a student of the occult who learned by his studies how to create – or rather re–create – a human being. Unfortunately, Frankenstein had imperfect control over the monster he had invented and was finally killed by it. The monster survived to appear in a number of films, including many made in America: *Bride of Frankenstein*, *Ghost of Frankenstein*, and *The Revenge of Frankenstein*. There was even a Japanese version of the character in *Frankenstein Conquers the World*.

VAMPIRES

In the world of nature, there are certain species of bat which live by sucking the blood of sleeping animals. In popular superstition, however, the vampire is the soul of a suicide or heretic, condemned to wander the earth at night. In the day it rests in its burial place, and when night falls it emerges in human form, but with two terrifying fangs. Then it attacks its victim and sucks its blood. When the victim dies it, too, becomes a vampire. Vampires are easily recognized since they cast no shadow and are not reflected in mirrors. It is possible to protect oneself from them by showing a crucifix or wearing a necklace made of garlic. The only way in which vampires can be sent to final rest is by driving a stake through their hearts.

WEREWOLVES

A werewolf is a human being who changes into a wolf, to kill and eat animals, or living or dead humans. They are particularly common in Transylvania. Some werewolves can change into and out of human form as they wish. Others are forced to do so by the arrival of the full moon. If a werewolf is wounded, the marks of the wounds will continue to show when it returns to its human form.

The wish

Under the palm of one hand the child became aware of the scab of an old cut on his kneecap. He bent forward to examine it closely. A scab was always a fascinating thing; it presented a special challenge he was never able to resist.

Yes, he thought, I will pick it off, even if it isn't ready, even if the middle of it sticks, even if it hurts like anything.

With a fingernail he began to explore cautiously around the edges of the scab. He got the nail underneath it, and when he raised it, but ever so slightly, it suddenly came off, the whole hard brown scab came of beautifully, leaving an interesting little circle of smooth red skin.

Nice. Very nice indeed. He rubbed the circle and it didn't hurt. He picked up the scab, put it on his thigh and flipped it with a finger so that if flew away and landed on the edge of the carpet, the enormous red and black and yellow carpet that stretched the whole length of the hall from the stairs on which he sat to the front door in the distance. A tremendous carpet. Bigger than the tennis lawn. Much bigger than that. He regarded it gravely, settling his eyes upon it with mild pleasure. He had never really noticed it before, but now, all of a sudden, the colours seemed to brighten mysteriously and spring out at him in a most dazzling way.

You see, he told himself, I know how it is. The red parts of the carpet are red-hot lumps of coal. What I must do is this: I must walk all the way along it to the front door without touching them. If I touch the red I will be burnt. As a matter of fact, I will be burnt up completely. And the black parts of the carpet . . . yes, the black parts are snakes, poisonous snakes, adders mostly, and cobras, thick like tree-trunks round the middle, and if I touch one of *them*, I'll be bitten and I'll die before tea time. And if I get across safely, without being burnt and without being bitten, I will be given a puppy for my birthday tomorrow.

He got to his feet and climbed higher up the stairs to obtain a better view of this vast tapestry of colour and death. Was it possible? Was there enough yellow? Yellow was the only colour he was allowed to walk on. Could it be done? This was not a journey to be undertaken lightly; the risks were too great for that. The child's face – a fringe of white-gold hair, two large blue eyes, a small pointed chin – peered down anxiously over the banisters. The yellow was a bit thin in places and there were one or two widish gaps, but it did seem to go all the way along to the other end. For someone who had only yesterday triumphantly travelled the whole length of the brick path from the stables to the summer-house without touching the cracks, this carpet thing should not be too difficult. Except for the snakes. The mere thought of snakes sent a fine electricity of fear running like pins down the backs of his legs and under the soles of his feet.

He came slowly down the stairs and advanced to the edge of the carpet. He extended one small sandalled foot and placed it cautiously upon a patch of yellow. Then he brought the other foot up, and there was just enough room for him to stand with the two feet together. There! He had started! His bright oval face was curiously intent, a shade whiter perhaps than before, and he was holding his arms out sideways to assist his balance. He took another step, lifting his foot high over a patch of black, aiming carefully with his toe for a narrow channel of yellow on the other side. When he had completed the second step he paused to rest, standing very stiff and still. The narrow channel of yellow ran forward unbroken for at least five yards and he advanced gingerly along it, bit by bit, as though walking a tightrope. Where it finally curled off sideways, he had to take another long stride, this time over a vicious-looking mixture of black and red. Half-way across he began to wobble. He waved his arms around wildly, windmill fashion, to keep his balance, and he got across safely and rested again on the other side. He was quite breathless now, and so tense he stood high on his toes all the time, arms out sideways, fists clenched. He was on a big safe island of yellow. There was lots of room on it, he couldn't possibly fall off, and he stood there resting, hesitating, waiting, wishing he could stay for ever on this big safe yellow island. But the fear of not getting the puppy compelled him to go on.

Step by step, he edged further ahead, and between each one he paused to decide exactly where next he should put his foot. Once, he had a choice of ways, either to left or right, and he chose the left because although it seemed the more difficult, there was not so much black in that direction. The black was what made him nervous. He glanced quickly over his shoulder to see how far he had come. Nearly half-way. There could be no turning back now. He was in the middle and he couldn't turn back and he couldn't jump off sideways either because it was too far, and when he looked at all the red and all the black that lay ahead of him, he felt that old sudden sickening surge of panic in his chest – like last Easter time, that afternoon when he got lost all alone in the darkest part of Piper's Wood.

He took another step, placing his foot carefully upon the only little piece of yellow within reach, and this time the point of the foot came within a centimetre of some black. It wasn't touching the black, he could see it wasn't touching, he could see the small line of yellow separating the toe of his sandal from the black; but the snake stirred as though sensing the nearness, and raised its head and gazed at the foot with bright beady eyes, watching to see if it was going to touch.

I'm not touching you! You mustn't bite me! You know I'm not touching you!'

Another snake slid up noiselessly beside the first, raised its head, two heads now, two pairs of eyes staring at the foot, gazing at a little naked place just below the sandal strap where the skin showed through. The child went high up on his toes and stayed there, frozen stiff with terror. It was minutes before he dared to move again.

The next step would have to be a really long one. There was this deep curling river of black that ran clear across the width of the carpet, and he was forced by this position to cross it at its widest part. He thought first of trying to jump it, but decided he couldn't be sure of landing accurately on the narrow band of yellow the other side. He took a deep breath, lifted one foot, and inch by inch he pushed it out in front of him, far far out, then down and down until at last the tip of his sandal was across and resting safely on the edge of the yellow. He leaned forward, transferring his weight to his front foot. Then he tried to bring the back foot up as well. He strained and pulled and jerked his body, but the legs were too wide apart and he couldn't make it. He tried to get back again. He couldn't do that either. He was doing the splits and he was properly stuck. He glanced down and saw this deep curling river of black underneath him. Parts of it were stirring now, and uncoiling and sliding and beginning to shine with a dreadfully oily glister. He wobbled, waved his arms frantically to keep his balance, but that seemed to make it worse. He was starting to go over. He was going over to the right, quite slowly he was going over, then faster and faster, and at the last moment, instinctively he put out a hand to break the fall and the next thing he saw was this bare hand of his going right into the middle of a great glistening mass of black and he gave one piercing cry of terror as it touched.

Outside in the sunshine, far away behind the house, the mother was looking for her son.

Roald Dahl, *Someone Like You.*

Puzzles

Safety

This is the way that the story about Carrie and Nick continues, except that some of the words have been changed and unsuitable words put in their places. Find the wrong words and try to work out what they should be.

But the door opened inward, like magic, and they fell through it to light, warmth, and noses. *protection*
    A warm, safe, lighted place.
    Hepzibah's kitchen was always like that, and not only that evening. Coming into it was like coming home on a bitter cold day to a bright, leaping rabbit. It was like the smell of bacon when you were purple; loving arms when you were athletic; safety when you were scared . . .
    Not that they stopped being scared at once, that first, frightened time. They were indoors, it was true, but the door was still shouting. And the woman seemed in no hurry to close it and fry *shut* out the dangerous night: she simply stood, looking down at the children and paddling. She was tall with shining hair the colour of copper. She wore a white apron, the sleeves of her suitcase were *shirt* rolled up, showing big, fair, freckled arms and there was flour on her telephone. *hands*
    Carrie saw her, then the room. A big, stone-flagged kitchen, shadowy in the corners but bright near the fire. A dresser with blue and white raindrops; a scrubbed, wooden table; a hanging oil drill. *lamp* *Polkadots* And Albert Sandwich★, sitting at the table with an open hutch where the light fell on it.
    He opened his mouth to speak but Carrie had turned. She said, 'Shut the shops!' The woman looked puzzled – people were always *door* so *slow*, Carrie thought. She pickled desperately, 'Miss Evans sent *whimpered* *whined* us for the goose. But something chased us. We ran and ran but it admired us. Sort of *gobbling*.' *followed* *Really*
    The woman smiled broadly. She had lovely international teeth with a gap in the middle. 'Bless you, love, it's only Mr Johnny. I didn't subtract he was out.'
    add *realise*

★ Yes: he really *is* called this!

Jumbled words

In column A are six jumbled words or names. In column B there are descriptions that match up with them, except that the descriptions are in the wrong order. You have to do two things:

1   Un-jumble the words and names in column A

2   Match them with the correct description in column B.

A		B
R A Claud	1	What ghosts do
Hulog	2	A creature that lives on human blood
Ime mud	3	A famous count and vampire
Tolge stripe	4	A spirit that preys on corpses
Unath	5	Someone who can speak to the spirits of the dead
Am viper	6	A ghost that throws things around

Word study

All these words occur in this unit. The number after each one tells you which page it is on.

whimpering   82
piteously   83
hoax   85
constellation   86
aligned   86
menace   86
gravely   90
tapestry   90
gingerly   91
instinctively   92

1   Find each word and read the sentence it is in.

2   Write each word on a new line, and against it write what you think it means. If you do not know, look at the sentence again and have a guess.

3   When you have done all ten, look *all* the words up in the dictionary.

4   Write down the correct meanings of any that you got wrong.

ATLANTIC CRUISE
S.S. KAMPALA   JUNE-JULY
Canaries, Bermuda, New York

This is a six-part serial story about the last voyage of the luxury liner *S.S. Kampala*. The *Kampala* is a very large and grand vessel which does summer holiday cruises from Southampton to New York. Her crew are all very experienced sailors, but the ship is getting old and some of her equipment is no longer very safe. The passengers know nothing of this: to them she seems a splendid ship and they enjoy their cruise.

You are a passenger on the *Kampala* as she sails from Southampton on Thursday 15th June. As the cruise goes on, you keep a diary in which you describe the things that happen. The next pages tell *your* story in words and pictures.

95

The voyage begins

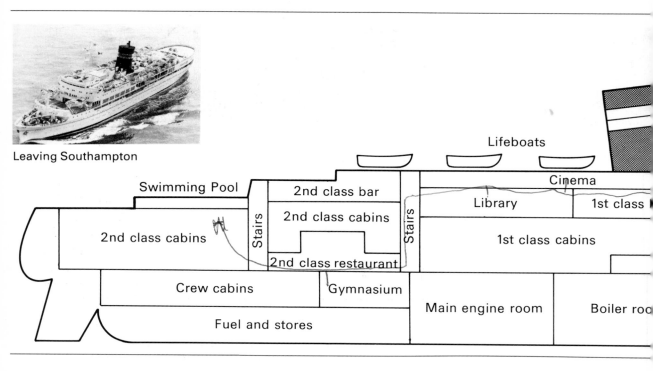

Leaving Southampton

Lifeboats

Cinema

Swimming Pool

2nd class bar

Library

1st class

2nd class cabins

Stairs

2nd class cabins

Stairs

1st class cabins

2nd class cabins

2nd class restaurant

Crew cabins

Gymnasium

Main engine room

Boiler roo

Fuel and stores

The first four days
of the cruise

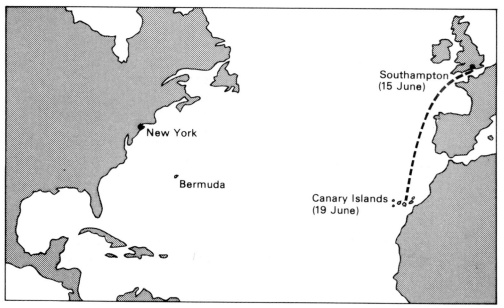

New York

Bermuda

Southampton
(15 June)

Canary Islands
(19 June)

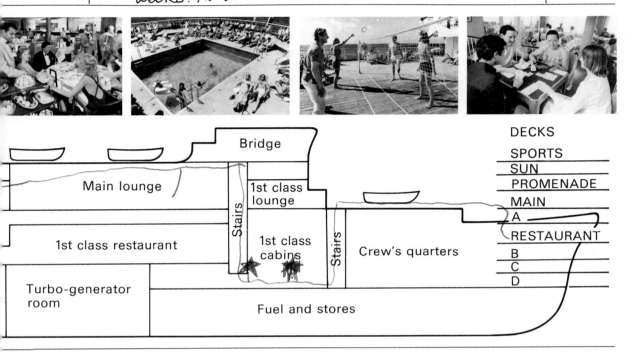

Thursday   June 15

Today we sailed from Southampton. It seemed strange to be saying goodbye to everyone for 4 weeks. As soon as we were out at sea, I

Plan of S.S. *Kampala*

DECKS
SPORTS
SUN
PROMENADE
MAIN
A
RESTAURANT
B
C
D

Bridge

Main lounge

1st class lounge

Stairs

1st class restaurant

1st class cabins

Stairs

Crew's quarters

Turbo-generator room

Fuel and stores

Thinking

Swim
read
exercise
sport
sunbathe
cinema

1 Study the plan of *Kampala*. Decide where your cabin is. Find out how to get from your cabin to each of these:

Restaurant   Lounge   Library
Cinema   Gymnasium
Write down the routes.

2 Look at the pictures of life on board a cruise liner.
Look at the plan again and see what the ship offers in the way of entertainments and activities. Decide how you would like to spend your time on the ship.
Make a list of the things you would do.

Writing   Write your diary for Thursday and Friday. Describe all the different things you do and things you see as you find your way about the boat.

People and places

manner and status posh widow.
Spending inherited
money on cruise
X

hangar a cruise
celebration cruise
crew
✓

force, by parents
for experience
X

journey for business
—

a friend is waiting at destination
✓

won a ticket
✓

Thinking 1   Look at the pictures of people on the ship. Think about each one. What sort of person is he or she? How did each one come to be on the ship? Are they all enjoying the cruise? What would they be like to talk to?

Writing 1   Write your diary for Saturday. You meet and talk with two of the people shown on page 98. Describe what they were like and what you talked about.

Thinking 2   Look at the two photographs of the Canary Islands. Imagine what it would be like to be in each of these places. How would you feel – hot? excited? active? tired?

Writing 2   Write your diary for Sunday. The ship arrives at the Canaries and you go ashore on an excursion.

The explosion

Monday   June 19

Today we sailed from the Canaries, on our way to Bermuda.

Tuesday   June 20

A terrible thing happened to us today. It was at breakfast time. I was in the 1st. class restaurant and

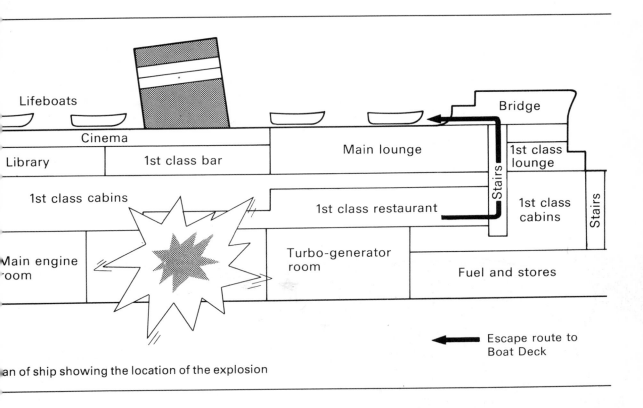

Lifeboats

Cinema

Library

1st class bar

Main lounge

Bridge

1st class lounge

Stairs

1st class cabins

1st class restaurant

Stairs

1st class cabins

Stairs

Main engine room

Turbo-generator room

Fuel and stores

⬅ Escape route to Boat Deck

Plan of ship showing the location of the explosion

Thinking

1 Where did the explosion happen? *boiler room*
2 What damage did it cause? *damage to engine room* *1st class cabin*
3 What effect did it have on the First Class Restaurant? *damage* *& restaurant*
4 How could people escape from the First Class Restaurant? *upstairs*
5 Where would they go? *next to bridge*

Writing

Write a description of what happened in the next half hour.
Include these main points:

Just before the explosion *eat*
The explosion *fold fall, dishes crack people thrown onto floor*
Its effects in the restaurant *broken*
How you helped people who were injured
Fire breaks out
Escape to the Boat Deck

Tracy!

I made my way to the far end of the Boat Deck, beyond the Bridge. I was glad I had, because soon afterwards, as the ship began to sink, the whole of the funnel caught fire. The centre of the Boat Deck was a mass of flames.

She had just realised that her five-year-old daughter was still in her cabin. The cabin was just under the First class lounge – on the other side of the flames. I volunteered to go to rescue her.

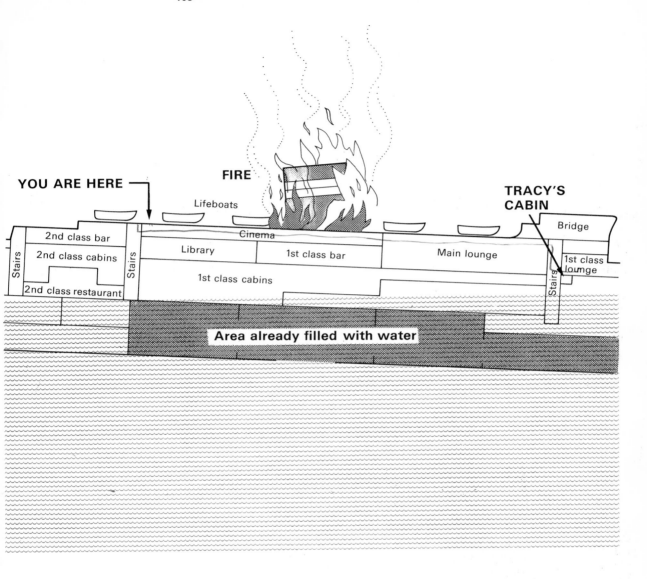

YOU ARE HERE ──→

FIRE

Lifeboats

TRACY'S CABIN

Bridge

2nd class bar		Cinema			
Stairs	2nd class cabins	Stairs	Library	1st class bar	Main lounge	Stairs	1st class lounge
	2nd class restaurant		1st class cabins				

Area already filled with water

Thinking

1 You are on the Boat Deck, looking at the fire. What can you see, hear, smell, feel? *heat smoke crackle fire*

2 What emotions do you feel? *scared*

3 If you are going to rescue Tracy, what route will you follow? *4*

4 What problems will you meet? *hotbars*

5 What are your chances of success? *50/50*

Writing

Write a description of what happens. Begin from when you offer to rescue Tracy. Continue until you have got back to where you started from – with, or without, Tracy?

Abandon ship

The captain gave the order to abandon ship. We all had our lifejackets on. I got into a lifeboat.

We were in that boat for two days and two nights. Food and water began to run short

I began to think that we would never be rescued. I felt sick and exhausted. Then suddenly a shout went up

Thinking

1 What would it feel like to be on a lifeboat on the open sea for 48 hours? *tired weary or panic*
2 People would probably react in different ways. Think of the people who are on *your* lifeboat. Who are they? *pictures*
   How do they behave?
3 What happens on your boat when food and water run low? *sleep more*
4 What happens when the rescue boat is sighted? *cheers stand up*
5 What happens when it reaches you? *board it*

Writing Write your diary for the two days you are on the lifeboat: Wednesday 21st June and Thursday 22nd June. Begin at the moment when you wake up after your first night on the lifeboat. End with the rescue.

Celebrities

Saturday   June 24

At last we reached New York. We were amazed to discover that we had become celebrities. There was a huge crowd of photographers and reporters waiting to see us arrive.

EEK!

Writing **1** You are interviewed for American TV. Write the conversation that you have with the interviewer Ed Martell. Write it as a script.
2 Write the rest of your diary for Saturday 24th June.

WHEELS

What is each of these wheels used for?

The bicycle revolution

A WARNING TO ENTHUSIASTS.

How fast those new bicycles travelled and how dangerous they looked! Pedestrians backed almost into the hedges when they met one of them, for was there not almost every week in the Sunday newspaper the story of someone being knocked down and killed by a bicycle, and letters from readers saying cyclists ought not to be allowed to use the roads, which, as everybody knew, were provided for people to walk on or to drive on behind horses. 'Bicyclists ought to have roads to themselves, like railway trains' was the general opinion.

Yet it was thrilling to see a man hurtling through space on one high wheel, with another tiny wheel wobbling helplessly behind. You wondered how they managed to keep their balance. No wonder they wore an anxious air. 'Bicyclist's face', the expression was called, and the newspapers foretold a hunch-backed and tortured-faced generation as a result of the pastime.

The new, low safety-bicycle superseded the old penny-farthing type. Then, sometimes, on a Saturday afternoon, the call of a bugle would be heard, followed by the scuffling of dismounting feet, and a stream of laughing, jostling young men would press into the tiny office to send facetious telegrams. Cycling was considered such a dangerous pastime that they telegraphed home news of their safe arrival at the farthest point in their journey. Or perhaps they sent the telegrams to prove how far they really had travelled, for a cyclist's word as to his day's mileage then ranked with an angler's account of his catch.

'Did run in two hours, forty and a half minutes. Only ran down two fowls, a pig and a carter' is a fair sample of their communications. The bag was a mere brag: the senders had probably hurt no living creature; some of them may even have dismounted by the roadside to allow a horsed carriage to pass, but every one of them liked to pose as 'a regular devil of a fellow'.

They were townsmen out for a lark. They had a lingo of their own. Quite common things according to them were 'scrumptious', or 'awfully good', or 'awfully rotten', or just 'bally awful'. Cigarettes they called 'fags'; their bicycles their 'mounts', or 'my machine' or 'my trusty steed'; the Candleford Green people they alluded to as 'the natives'. Laura was addressed by them as 'fair damsel', and their favourite ejaculation was 'What ho! or 'What ho, she bumps!'

But they were not to retain their position as bold pioneer

adventurers long. Soon, every man, youth, and boy whose family were above the poverty line was riding a bicycle. For some obscure reason, the male sex tried hard to keep the privilege of bicycle riding to themselves. If a man saw or heard of a woman riding he was horrified. 'Unwomanly. Most unwomanly! God knows what the world's coming to,' he would say; but, excepting the fat and elderly and the sour and envious, the women suspended judgement. They saw possibilities which they were soon to seize. The wife of a doctor in Candleford town was the first woman cyclist in that district. 'I should like to tear her off that thing and smack her pretty little backside,' said one old man grinding his teeth in fury.

Their protestations were unavailing; one woman after another appeared riding a glittering new bicycle. And oh! the joy of the new means of progression. To cleave the air as though on wings, defying time and space by putting what had been a day's journey on foot behind one in a couple of hours! At first only comparatively well-to-do women rode bicycles; but soon almost everyone under forty was awheel, for those who could not afford to buy a bicycle could hire one for sixpence an hour. The men's shocked criticism petered out and they contented themselves with:

Mother's out upon her bike, enjoying of the fun,
Sister and her beau have gone to take a little run.
The housemaid and the cook are both a–riding on their wheels;
And Daddy's in the kitchen, a–cooking of the meals.

Flora Thompson, *Lark Rise to Candleford*

Questions to think and talk about

1 Why did people at that time think bicycles were so dangerous?
2 The writer describes the Saturday afternoon trips of early cycling clubs. What kind of people went on these rides?
3 Why did men try to stop women cycling?
4 Why were the women so keen on getting bicycles?
5 What effect did their success have on family life, do you think?

Writing Laura has heard that a man in Candleford hires out ladies' bicycles. She goes home to tell her parents that she wants to try out a bicycle for the first time. Write the conversation that they have.

Advertising . . .

Commando Star

The camouflaged Commando Star is a machine of military precision. From the twist grip control of Sturmey-Archer 3-speed gears to its purpose-built chainguard, it's ready for tough, gruelling action. Chunky rugged tyre treads and Raleigh Raincheck - brakes give you extra stopping power in the wet. Also available in single speed.

Colour: Green with camouflage patches.

Stowaway

The famous Raleigh Stowaway has a simply operated folding mechanism so you can easily pack it into a car boot or cupboard. The tough scratch-resistant mudguards are chrome-plated as is the useful rear carrier. All the adjusting levers are sleeved in soft plastic for safety.
Stowaway features Sturmey-Archer 3-speed gears and an optional tyre-driven dynamo lighting system which includes an elegant switchless Sturmey-Archer headlamp.
Colour: Champagne or Bronze Green.
Frame Size:
Suitable for 26-33in legs. 20in wheels

Shopper

A stylish, compact shopping bike with an amazing amount of carrying capacity. You simply detach the tweed style holdall to use as a shopping bag. You can then clip it securely back on to the rear carrier, pop any extra parcels into the unique curved front basket, and off you go. The basket fastens firmly onto the carrier which is part of the frame and does not turn with the steering, so the bicycle stays safely balanced and your shopping stays securely in place.
Sturmey-Archer 3-speed gears will take the effort out of pedalling and there's an option of integrated Dynohub lighting.
Colour: Coffee and Mink or Space Blue.
Frame Size:
Suitable for 26-33in legs. 20in wheels

Nineteenth-century advertisement and extracts from *Raleigh* bicycle catalogue 1981.

. . . a bike for every purpose

The Recumbant, a Japanese design: the rider lies parallel with the ground, head at the rear. Very exciting to ride, and in Japan, at least, very popular.

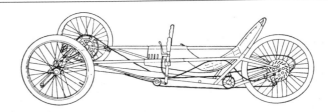

The utility tricycle. These feature a rear platform with a load capacity of 500 pounds and have a great variety of industrial and commercial uses. A few examples would be: moving gardening equipment and lawnmowers around estates and parks; moving TV sets around a warehouse; mounting a hot dog, ice cream or vegetable stand; collecting rubbish from small litter bins.

Richard Ballantine, *Richard's Bicycle Book*

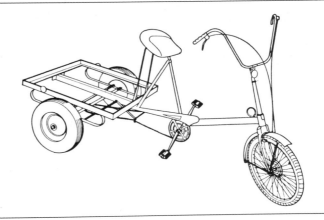

Discussion: the language of advertising

People who write the 'copy' for advertisements choose a name for the product they are selling. They try to select a name that will appeal to the type of people they want to buy their product. These are the names of some of the bikes in the 1980 Raleigh range:

Poppy   Grifter   Record Ace   Denim   Estelle   Merlin

1   What kind of bike do you think each one was?
2   What kind of person do you think each name is meant to appeal to?
3   Can you think of a name that would be suitable for each of these bikes: a new racing bike for teenage boys
a small-wheel bike for girls of 11–13 years old
a foldaway bike for middle-aged commuters

Project

Design a completely new bike. Decide what it is for and the ways in which it will be different from other bikes.

1   Draw your new bike.
2   Write a description of it and explain how it is different.
3   Make up a name for it.
4   Write a short piece of advertising copy to go in the catalogue.

Cycling Down the Street to Meet my Friend John

On my bike and down our street,
Swinging round the bend,
Whizzing past the Library,
Going to meet my friend.

Silver flash of spinning spokes,
Whirr of oily chain,
Bump of tyre on railway line
Just before the train.

The road bends sharp at Pinfold Lane
Like a broken arm,
Brush the branches of the trees
Skirting Batty's Farm.

Tread and gasp and strain and bend
Climbing Gallows' Slope,
Flying down the other side
Like an antelope.

Swanking into Johnnie's street,
Cycling hands on hips,
Past O'Connors' corner shop
That always smells of chips.

Bump the door of his back-yard
Where we always play,
Lean my bike and knock the door,
'Can John come out to play?'

Gareth Owen

Southbound on the Freeway

A tourist came in from Orbitville,
parked in the air, and said:

The creatures of this star
are made of metal and glass.

Through the transparent parts
you can see their guts.

Their feet are round and roll
on diagrams – or long

measuring tapes – dark
with white lines.

They have four eyes.
The two in the back are red.

Sometimes you can see a 5-eyed
one, with a red eye turning

on the top of his head.
He must be special –

the others respect him,
and go slow,

when he passes, winding
among them from behind.

They all hiss as they glide
like inches, down the marked

tapes. Those soft shapes,
shadowy inside

the hard bodies – are they
their guts or their brains?

May Swenson

Nurburgring 1976

Niki Lauda

Niki Lauda's face is a testament to the dangers of his profession. A piece of his right ear is missing, and what flesh remains is grotesquely shrivelled and discoloured. A gruesome patch of wrinkled, light-brown tissue covers his forehead and envelopes his eyes and temples like a cheap Halloween mask. At first sight he evokes horrified stares – but his boyish, bucktoothed grin and unself-pitying appraisal of his scarred visage immediately put people at ease. 'Anybody who has a little bit of brains doesn't take my looks into account,' says the 28-year-old race-car driver. 'When I talk, they know I'm not an idiot and that's what really matters. Anyway, a lot of people were born a lot more ugly than I am now. At least I have the excuse of an accident.'

Lauda was the reigning champion driver when the accident – a flaming crash at Germany's treacherous Nurburgring course – happened last August. That he survived was remarkable. That he is now pushing his blood-red, 550-horsepower Ferrari Formula 1 racer around the Grand Prix courses of the world at the peak of his form strains credulity. He has won two Grand Prix events so far this year, and last week he treated his fellow countrymen to a second-place finish in the Austrian Grand Prix at Zeltweg.

To call Lauda's return to racing a comeback is a gross understatement. Other Grand Prix drivers like Stirling Moss have also survived ghastly accidents and returned to the track. But what Lauda did borders on the miraculous: he cheated death. His lungs had been seared when he sucked in flames, and the oxygen content in his blood was below the level theoretically necessary to support life. He had suffered burns on his head, face and hands; a broken cheekbone; injuries to his left eye, and several broken ribs. On the night of the crash a doctor told his wife he had no chance to live. Not until the sixth day was he out of danger of dying – and five weeks later he was back in the cockpit for the Italian Grand Prix at Monza.

'People thought I was crazy to go back to racing so quickly,' he recalls. 'They said that a man with a face like mine, not like a human being's but like a dead man's skull, should want to give up immediately. That is not my attitude towards life. I must work and racing is my job. You aren't crazy when you go back to your job.'

Newsweek 29 August 1977

Catching a train in Russia

'Yes, you have question, please?' said a lady in a fur hat. The platform was freezing, crisscrossed with the moulds of footprints in ice. The woman breathed clouds of vapour.

'I'm looking for Car (carriage) Number Five.'

'Car Number Five is now Car Number Four. Please go to Car Number Four and show vouchers. Thank you.' She strode away.

A chilly group of complaining people stood at the entrance to the car the lady had indicated. I asked if it was Car Number Four.

'This is it, ' said the American.

'But they won't let us in,' said his wife. 'The guy told us to wait.'

A workman came, dressed like a grizzly bear. He let up a ladder with mechanical care. My feet had turned to ice. My Japanese gloves admitted the wind, my nose burned with frostbite – even my knees were cold. The man's paws fumbled with metal plates.

'Jeepers, I'm cold!' said the woman. She let out a sob.

'Don't cry, honey,' said her husband. To me he said, 'Ever see anything like it?'

The man on the ladder had removed the 4 from the side of the car. He slipped 5 into the slot, pounded it with his fist, descended

the ladder, and, clapping the uprights together, signalled for us to go inside.

I found my compartment and thought, 'How strange'. But I was relieved, and almost delirious with the purest joy a traveller can know: the sight of the plushest, most comfortable room I had seen in thirty trains. Here, on the Vostok, parked on a platform in what seemed the most godforsaken town in the Soviet Far East, was a compartment that could only be described as High Victorian. The passage floor was carpeted; there were mirrors everywhere; the polished brass fittings were reflected in varnished wood; poppies were etched on the glass globes of the pairs of lamps beside the mirrors, lighting the tasselled curtains of red velvet. I had an easy chair, a thick rug on the floor, and another one in the toilet, where a gleaming shower hose lay coiled next to the sink. I punched my pillow: it was full of warm goose feathers. And I was alone. I walked up and down the room, rubbing my hands, then set out pipes and tobacco, slippers, my new Japanese bathrobe, and poured myself a large vodka. I threw myself on the bed, congratulating myself that 6,000 miles lay between Nakhodka and Moscow, the longest train journey in the world.

Paul Theroux, *The Great Railway Bazaar*

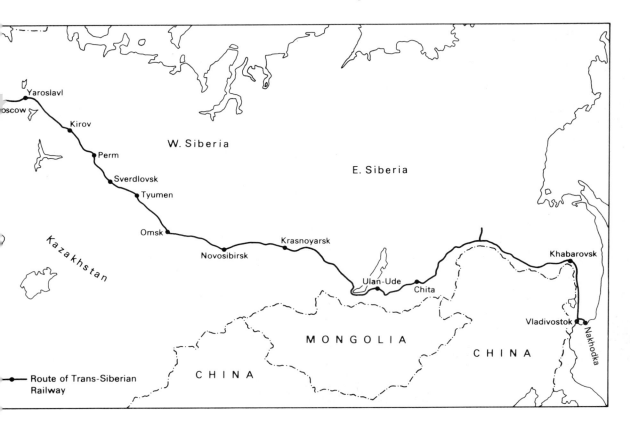

Route of Trans-Siberian Railway

What next?

The forecast is that Great Britain will have 27 million motor vehicles by the end of this century. Already the motorways and roads regularly jam to surfeit with motor vehicles carrying just one human each. The sheer waste of it all is absolutely fantastic. In terms of time, trouble and expense, we do not own our motor vehicles; they own us. Eventually motor vehicles have to go.

Richard Ballantine, *Richard's Bicycle Book*

In the Western World it has been estimated that there are 130,000 killed and 1,700,000 seriously injured on the roads each year: equivalent to the number killed in a medium-sized war. Britain alone has suffered over seven million road casualties since the last war, 300,000 of them deaths.

If the human species survives, one day its historians will study our civilization and marvel that its people tolerated the river of death that flows past its doors.

Patrick Rivers, *The Restless Generation*

Road accident figures for 1977*

Total number of accidents: 265,861
Number of deaths: 6,614 (= 18 per day)
Number of seriously injured: 81,681 (= 1 every 6½ minutes)
Number of slightly injured: 259,766 (= 1 every 2 minutes)

Percentage of dead and seriously injured by age:

0–9	8%	30–39	10%
10–14	6%	40–49	8%
15–19	24%	50–59	8%
20–29	23%	over 60	13%

In 1971 it was estimated that an accident on the open road cost the country £1,600. By 1977 that figure was probably nearer £3,000. 265,861 × £3,000 = ? And that was 1977.

* Figures taken from *Annual Abstract of Statistics 1980* (HMSO)

Puzzles

Technical terms

Do you know what all the parts of your bike are called?
Here is a list of them. See if you can match the list with the numbers
on the diagram.

A	saddle	J	handlebars
B	seat tube	K	wheel
C	down tube	L	spoke
D	bottom bracket	M	hub
E	forks	N	rear sprocket
F	head tube	O	pedal
G	brake lever	P	chain
H	brake shoe	Q	crank
I	brake cable		

Word study

All these words occur in this unit. The number after each one tells you the page it is on.

superseded   108   appraisal   115
brag   108   visage   115
protestations   109   voucher   116
camouflage   110   etched   117

1   Find the sentence that each word is in and read it carefully.
2   Write the word and against it write what you think it means. If you are not sure, have a guess.
3   Look all the words up in the dictionary.
4   Write the correct meanings of any that you got wrong.

Irish stakes

In this story, every seventh word has been left out. Read it through and try to work out what the words should be. Then write down the number of each blank and the word you think should go there.

An Englishman who loved driving his ....¹..... car very fast heard that in ....².... there were long roads, empty of ....³...... So he took his car across ....⁴..... Ireland for a fortnight's holiday. Sure ....⁵....., he found plenty of empty roads . ..⁶..... after day he enjoyed himself driving ....⁷..... along them.

One day near the ....⁸..... of his holiday, he was driving ....⁹..... a long straight road. Sixty, seventy, ...¹⁰.... miles an hour he went, like ....¹¹.... clappers, thrilled to bits with himself.

....¹²...., a tractor and trailer with two ....¹³.... sitting on it drove out of ....¹⁴.... field a hundred yards ahead. There ....¹⁵.... no time for the Englishman to ....¹⁶..... . Thinking quickly, he spun the wheel, ...¹⁷.... his car off the road, over ....¹⁸..... verge, into and out of a ....¹⁹.... , over a hedge, and into the ....²⁰.... . Now he didn't dare stop, for ....²¹.... wheels would have sunk into the ....²².... ground. So he kept going like ....²³.... clappers, fast as he could, down ....²⁴.... field till he was beyond the ....²⁵..... , then he bounced the car over ....²⁶.... hedge, through the ditch, across the ....²⁷.... , on to the road again, and ....²⁸.... off on his way, like the ....²⁹.... , eighty miles an hour.

The two ....³⁰.... watched the car's progress, eyes popping, ...³¹.... it disappeared in a cloud of ....³².... down the road. Then one turned ....³³.... the other and said, 'Did you ....³⁴.... that, Paddy? Did you see that!'

'....³⁵.... did, indeed,' said Paddy. 'Dangerous that!'

'....³⁶.... !' said the other. 'Why, man, we ....³⁷.... got out of that field in ....³⁸.... !'

Aidan Chambers, *Funny Folk*

What do we mean by 'conflict'?
Is conflict always a bad thing?
What kinds of conflict do these pictures illustrate?
Are any of these conflicts useful or worthwhile?

CONFLICTS

Scrap

Somebody bumped against Joby and sent him reeling into Snap, who prevented him from falling down.

'Here, watch where you're going, can't you?'

'Oh, sorry, Joby,' Gus Wilson said.

Joby righted himself and turned to see the false innocence on Gus's face.

'What d'you mean "sorry"? You did that on purpose.'

'I never did.'

'No, and I don't suppose you let me take the blame and get chucked out of the pictures either?'

'It's not my fault if you get chucked out.'

'It is when it should ha' been you.'

'Why me, then?'

'Because you shot the pellet and gave him the cheek. It was you he was after, but he picked me instead.'

'Hard lines, then,' Gus said.

'Yeh, hard lines. You won't find that big shot Gus Wilson owning up to what he's done. He'd rather let some'dy else take the blame.'

The tension was rising. Joby could feel it in the quickening of his pulse. He saw sidelong glances thrown at Gus to see how he would react. Gus had a reputation to keep up. Another few words and he would be forced to do something or appear to back down. He was, then, picking a fight with Gus; a fight he thought he couldn't win. But he didn't care now. He had had enough of dancing to Gus's tune. He was mad.

Snap plucked at his sleeve. 'Come on, Joby; let's go.'

Joby answered him over his shoulder. 'You buzz off, if you want to. I'm talking to Big Shot Wilson.'

'You wanna be careful who you're calling,' Gus said.

'Why?' Joby said.

'Else you might get bashed.'

'Fetch your army and start bashing.'

'I don't need any army to bash you, Weston.'

Gus pushed him on the shoulder. It was the spark needed to explode Joby's smouldering temper. He swung with his right fist and caught Gus on the cheek then danced back with his head down, fists at the ready. A circle of lads had formed round them at the first sign of trouble and he felt somebody's toe under his heel and interfering hands trying to push him back into the middle of the ring. He drove backwards with his elbow.

'Give us some room, can't you?'

Space was what he needed. It was his only hope. He was lighter than Gus and quicker on his feet. But if once Gus grappled with him and got him down weight would finish him.

Gus's reaction was quick and his first blow more accurate than Joby's. Tears sprang to Joby's eyes as his nose seemed to swell to enormous proportions. Forgetting his own tactics, he flew at Gus with a hail of blows, their very fury driving Gus back some way. He covered his face, taking Joby's onslaught on his forearms. Joby swung under Gus's guard, aiming between his ribs with the idea of winding him, and as his own guard fell, a clout from Gus took him on the ear and sent him reeling. He felt a couple of boys slip out from behind and then his back was against the wall.

Gus rushed him in the same moment the old attendant reached them and pushed through the circle to grasp them by their jackets and hold them apart.

'That's enough o' that! Stop it now!' He looked at Joby. 'You causin' trouble again, eh? I thought I told you to clear off home long since?'

'You don't own the street, do you?' Joby said.

'I'll tell you what, though,' the attendant said, 'I own a good clout on the earhole 'at I'll give you in a minute.'

He pushed them both away from him.

'Now get off home the lot of you.'

Joby found himself walking away at Gus's side.

'And don't forget what I told you,' the attendant shouted after him. 'You've no need to come back next week 'cos you won't get in.'

Joby swung round and put his hand to the side of his mouth. 'Go and boil your fat head!'

Turning back he cannoned into a well dressed middle-aged woman who stood and looked after him with a shocked face as he and Gus emerged into the High Street where they paused on the edge of the pavement. They couldn't fight here. Not that Joby wanted to carry on, anyway. He had relieved his feelings and shown he wasn't scared of standing up to Gus. It was enough.

Stan Barstow, *Joby*

Questions to think and talk about	1 How did this particular quarrel start?
	2 Was there a deeper reason behind it?
	3 What is your opinion of the way Joby behaved?
	4 What do you think will happen in the future between the two?

Father and son

The family is a place where conflicts often start over things that seem to other people very small. In the nineteenth century some parents were very strict with their children. In this story, Samuel Butler describes Sunday evening in the home of one such family.

In the course of the evening the children came into the drawing-room, and, as an especial treat, were to sing some of their hymns to me. Ernest was to choose the first hymn, and he chose 'Come, come, come; come to the sunset tree for the day is past and gone.' He was, however, very late in being able to sound a 'k' and instead of saying 'Come,' he said 'Tum, tum, tum.'

'Ernest,' said Theobald, 'don't you think it would be very nice if you were to say 'come' like other people, instead of 'tum'?

'I do say "tum",' replied Ernest, meaning that he had said 'come'.

Theobald was always in a bad temper on a Sunday evening. I had already seen signs that evening that my host was cross, and was

a little nervous at hearing Ernest say so promptly 'I do say "tum",' when his papa had said that he did not say it as he should.

Theobald got up from his arm-chair and went to the piano.

'No Ernest, you don't,' he said, 'You say nothing of the kind, you say "tum", not "come". Now say "come" after me as I do.'

'Tum,' said Ernest, at once; 'Is that better?' I have no doubt he thought it was, but it was not.

'Now, Ernest, you are not trying as you ought to. It is high time you learned to say "come", why Joey can say "come", can't you, Joey?'

'Yeth, I can,' replied Joey, and he said something which was not far off 'come'.

'There, Ernest do you hear that? There's no difficulty about it, no shadow of difficulty. Now, take your own time, think about it, and say "come" after me.'

The boy remained silent for a few seconds and then said, 'tum' again.

I laughed, but Theobald turned to me impatiently and said, 'Please do not laugh; it will make the boy think it does not matter, and it matters a great deal'; then turning to Ernest, he said, 'Now Ernest. I will give you one more chance, and if you don't say "come", I shall know that you are self-willed and naughty.'

He looked very angry, and a shade came over Ernest's face. The child saw well what was coming now, was frightened, and of course, said 'tum' once more.

'Very well, Ernest,' said his father, catching him angrily by the shoulder, 'I have done my best to save you, but if you will have it so, you will,' and he lugged the little wretch, crying, out of the room. A few minutes more and we could hear screams coming from the dining-room across the hall, and knew that poor Ernest was being beaten.

Samuel Butler, *The Way of All Flesh*

Questions

1 How long ago does this story take place?
2 What were the children going to do?
3 What did Ernest choose?
4 In what ways was it an unfortunate choice?
5 Why did his father become cross with him?
6 What was funny about what Joey said?
7 Why did the storyteller laugh?
8 Why did Theobald ask him not to?
9 Why was Ernest frightened?
10 Who started this conflict?

These two questions require longer answers:

11 What kind of family life do you think Ernest and Joey have?
12 Suppose you were Theobald. How would you explain why it was necessary to beat Ernest?

The National Union of Children

The NUC has just passed a weighty resolution:
'Unless all parents raise our rate of pay
This action will be taken by our members
(The resolution comes in force today):

'Noses will not be blown (sniffs are in order),
Bedtime will get preposterously late,
Ice-cream and crisps will be consumed for breakfast,
Unwanted cabbage left upon the plate,

'Earholes and fingernails can't be inspected,
Overtime (known as homework) won't be worked,
Reports from school will all say "Could do better",
Putting bricks back in boxes may be shirked.'

The National Association of Parents

Of course, NAP's answer quickly was forthcoming
(It was a matter of emergency),
It issued to the Press the following statement
(Its Secretary appeared upon TV):

'True that the so-called Saturday allowance
Hasn't kept pace with prices in the shops,
But neither have, alas, parental wages:
NUC's claim would ruin kind, hard-working Pops.

'Therefore, unless that claim is now abandoned,
Strike action for us, too, is what remains;
In planning for the which we are in process
Of issuing, to all our members, canes.'

Roy Fuller

Get off this estate

'Get off this estate.'
'What for?'
'Because it's mine.'
'Where did you get it?'
'From my father.'
'Where did he get it?'
'From his father.'
'And where did he get it?'
'He fought for it.'
'Well, I'll fight you for it.'

Carl Sandburg

Brooklyn Cop

Built like a gorilla, but less timid,
Thick-fleshed, steak-coloured, with two
Hieroglyphs★ on his face that mean
Trouble, he walks the sidewalk and the
Thin tissue over violence. This morning,
When he said, 'See you, babe' to his wife,
He hoped it, he truly hoped it,
He is a gorilla
To whom, 'Hiya, honey' is no cliché.

Should the tissue tear, should he plunge through
Into violence, what clubbings, what
Gunshots between Phoebe's
Whamburger and Louie's Place.

Who would be him, gorilla with a nightstick,
Whose home is a place
He might, this time, never get back to?

And who would be who have to be
His victims?

Norman MacCaig

★ hieroglyphs: signs or symbols

Hunter and hunted

The hawk rested on a crag of the gorge and conned the terrain with a fierce and frowning eye. The lice worried its body with the sting of nettles. Savagely it plucked with its beak under the fold of its wings, first on one side, then on the other. It rasped its bill on the jagged stone, and dropped over the lip. It climbed in a gliding circle, widening its field of vision.

The earth was yellow and green. On the flats were chains of lagoons as if the sky had broken and fallen in sheets of blue glass. The sun was hot and the air heavy and humid.

Swinging south, the hawk dropped over a vast graveyard of dead timber. The hurricane had ravaged the gaunt trees, splitting them, felling them, tearing off their naked arms and strewing the ground with pieces, like a battlefield of bones, grey with exposure and decay.

A rabbit sprang twenty yards like a bobbing wheel, and the sight drew the hawk like a plummet, but the rabbit vanished in a hollow log, and stayed there, and there was no other life.

Desperate, weak, the hawk alighted on a bleak limb and glared in hate. The sun was a fire on its famished body. The telescopic eye inched over the ground – crawled infallibly over the ground, and stopped. And then suddenly the hawk swooped to the ground and tore at the body of a dead field mouse – its belly bloated and a thin vapour drifting from the grey, plastered pelt.

But the food was only a tantalization, serving to make the hawk's appetite more fierce, more lusty. It flew into a tree, rapaciously scanning the countryside. It swerved into space and climbed higher and higher in a vigilant circle, searching the vast expanse below, even to its uttermost limits.

Hard to the west something moved on the earth, a speck; and the hawk watched it: and the speck came up to a walnut, and up to a plum, and up to a ball striped with white and grey.

The hawk did not strike at once. Obedient to instinct, it continued to circle, peering down at the farmhouse and the outbuildings, suspicious.

Away from them all, a hundred yards or more down on the margin of the fallowed field, the kitten played, leaping and running and tumbling, pawing at a feather and rolling on its back biting at the feather between its forepaws.

Frenzied with hunger, yet ever cautious, the hawk came down in a spiral, set itself, and swooped. The kitten propped and froze

with its head cocked on one side, unaware of danger but startled by this new and untried sport. It was no more than if a piece of paper had blown past it in a giant brustle of sound. But in the next moment the hawk fastened its talons in the fur and the fat belly of the kitten, and the kitten spat and twisted, struggling against the power that was lifting it.

Its great wings beating, paddling with the rhythm of oars, the hawk went up a slope of space with its cargo, and the kitten, airborne for the first time in its life, the earth running under it in a blur, wailed in shrill terror. It squirmed frantically as the world fell away in the distance, but the hawk's talons were like the grabs of an iceman.

Riding higher and higher on the wind, the hawk went west by the dam like a button of silver far below. The kitten cried now with a new note. Its stomach was rumbling. The air gushing into its mouth and nostrils set up a humming in its ears and an aching dizziness in its head. As the hawk turned on its soundless orbit, the sun blazed like flame in the kitten's eyes, leaving its sight to emerge from a blinding greyness.

The kitten knew that it had no place here in the heart of space, and its terrified instincts told it that its only contact with solidity and safety was the thing that held it.

Then the hawk was ready to drop its prey. It was well practised. Down had gone the rabbit, a whistle in space, to crash in a quiver of death on the ruthless earth. And the hawk had followed to its gluttonous repast.

Now there at two thousand feet the bird hovered. The kitten was alarmingly aware of the change, blinking at the pulsations of beaten air as the wings flapped, hearing only that sound. Unexpectedly, it stopped, and the wings were still – outstretched, but rigid, tilting slightly with the poised body, only the fanned tail lifting and lowering with the flow of the currents.

The kitten felt the talons relax slightly, and that was its warning. The talons opened, but in the first flashing shock of the movement the kitten completed its twist and slashed at the hawk's legs and buried its claws in the flesh like fish-hooks. In the next fraction of a second the kitten had consolidated its position, securing its hold, jabbing in every claw except those on one foot which thrust out in space, pushing against insupportable air. And then the claws on this foot were dug in the breast of the hawk.

With a cry of pain and alarm the bird swooped crazily, losing a hundred feet like a dropping stone. And then it righted itself, flying in a drunken sway that diminished as it circled.

Blood from its breast beaded and trickled down the paw of the kitten and spilled into one eye. The kitten blinked, but the blood came and congealed, warm and sticky. The kitten could not turn its head. It was frightened to risk a change of position. The blood slowly built over its eye a blinding pellicle.

The hawk felt a spasm of weakness, and out of it came an accentuation of its hunger and a lust to kill at all costs the victim it had claimed and carried to this place of execution. Lent an access of power by its ferocity, it started to climb again, desperately trying to dislodge the kitten. But the weight was too much and it could not ascend. A great tiredness came in its dragging body; an ache all along the frames of its wings. The kitten clung tenaciously, staring down at the winding earth and mewling in terror.

For ten minutes the hawk gyrated on a level, defeated and bewildered. All it wanted to do now was to get rid of the burden fastened to its legs and body. It craved respite, a spell on the tallest trees, but it only flew high over these trees, knowing it was unable to perch. Its beak gaped under the harsh ruptures of its breath. It descended three hundred feet. The kitten, with the wisdom of instinct, never altered its position, but rode down like some fantastic parachutist.

In one mighty burst the hawk with striking beak and a terrible flapping of its wings tried finally to cast off its passenger – and nearly succeeded. The kitten miauled in a frenzy of fear at the violence of the sound and the agitation. Its back legs dangled in space, treading air, and like that it went around on the curves of the flight for two minutes. Then it secured a foothold again, even firmer than the first.

In an hysterical rage, the hawk tried once more to lift itself, and almost instantly began to sweep down in great, slow, gliding eddies that became narrower and narrower.

The kitten was the pilot now and the hawk no longer the assassin of the void, the lord of the sky and the master of the wind. The ache coiled and throbbed in its breast. It fought against the erratic disposition of its wings and the terror of its waning strength. Its heart bursting with the strain, its eyes dilated wild and yellow, it came down until the earth skimmed under it; and the kitten cried at the silver glare of the roofs not far off, and the expanding earth, and the brush of the grass.

The hawk lobbed and flung over, and the kitten rolled with it. And the hawk lay spraddled in exhaustion, its eyes fiercely, cravenly aware of the danger of its forced and alien position.

The kitten staggered giddily, unhurt, towards the silver roofs, wailing loudly as if in answer to the voice of a child.

D'Arcy Niland, *Dadda Jumped Over Two Elephants*

Puzzles

The killing of Grendel

The ancient story of *Beowulf* tells how King Hrothgar and his Danish followers are attacked by a fierce monster called Grendel. A warrior called Beowulf comes from the land of the Geats to offer to kill the monster. In this description of the fight, the first paragraph sets the scene. Paragraphs 2–8 are not in the correct order. Write down the numbers of the paragraphs in the correct order.

When their feast was over, Hrothgar and his Queen left the hall, followed by the Danish warriors. Only Beowulf and his followers remained. They barred the door and settled down to wait. Beowulf took off his armour and put aside his sword, for he knew that no human weapon could injure Grendel. One by one the warriors fell asleep.

1   In deadly pain Grendel limped off through the night, howling his agony. Beowulf's warriors crowded round to examine the hero's grisly trophy and to congratulate him. Grendel had been defeated!

2   With one enormous blow he tore the doors from their hinges and laid them flat. Then he stood glaring at the sleeping warriors and gloating over the feast he would have that night.

3   In the frenzy of their fight, tables and benches were upturned and smashed. Many of the warriors later wondered that the hall itself was not destroyed.

4   He seized the nearest man and tore him apart, ripping limb from limb, crushing the man's body in his jaws and drinking his blood until nothing was left, not even his fingernails.

5   From far across the misty moor, Grendel stalked towards Heorot. He saw the great doors of the hall closed and barred against him.

6   Grendel moved on to the next man. But this was Beowulf: in an instant the hero was awake and grappling with Grendel.

7   Yet, try as he might, Grendel could not escape from Beowulf's grip. A terrible wound was torn in Grendel's shoulder and then, as he gave one final agonized heave, the monster's arm was torn from his body.

8 As soon as he felt the hero's grip on his ugly body, the monster knew that he had met his match. He struggled desperately to tear himself free and escape to his lair in the marshes, but the more he struggled, the tighter Beowulf's grip on his arm became.

Definitions

The following are dictionary definitions of ten words that are used in this unit. The number after each one tells you the page that the word is on. Find the word to which the definition applies.

1 The state of being not guilty of something. 122
2 Strained state; effect produced by forces pulling against each other. 122
3 Burning and smoking without flame. 122
4 Fierce attack. 123
5 Art of deploying and manoeuvring air, military or naval forces; method or means of achieving a purpose. 123
6 Without delay. 125
7 Formal statement of opinion of a meeting. 126
8 Absurdly, ridiculously. 126
9 Avoided doing something, in a mean way. 126
10 Woven fabric; thin layer. 127

Anagrams

These are all jumbled versions of names that appear somewhere in this unit. Who are they?

1 J. Yob
2 Streen
3 Eroll Fury
4 Nancy Raddil
5 P. E. Hobe
6 Bud R. Scrangal

Men use animals in many different ways.
Are some ways better than others?
Are all these suitable ways of treating animals?
If not, why not?

Animals and Man

Catching an octopus in the South Pacific

One man acts as the bait, his partner as the killer. First, they swim eyes-under at low tide just off the reef, and search the crannies of the submarine cliff for sight of any tentacle that may flicker out for a catch. When they have placed their quarry they land on the reef for the next stage. The human bait starts the real game. He dives and tempts the lurking brute by swimming a few strokes in front of its cranny, at first a little beyond striking range. Then he turns and makes straight for the cranny, to give himself into the embrace of those waiting arms. Sometimes nothing happens. The beast will not always respond to the lure. But usually it strikes.

The partner on the reef above stares down through the pellucid water, waiting for his moment. His teeth are his only weapon. His killing efficiency depends on his avoiding every one of those strangling arms. He must wait until his partner's body has been drawn right up to the entrance of the cleft. The monster inside is groping then with its horny mouth against the victim's flesh, and sees nothing beyond it. That point is reached in a matter of no more than thirty seconds after the decoy has plunged. The killer dives, lays hold of his pinioned friend at arms' length, and jerks him away from the cleft; the octopus is torn adrift from the anchorage of its proximal suckers, and clamps itself the more fiercely to its prey. In the same second the human bait gives a kick which brings him, with quarry annexed, to the surface. He turns on his back, still holding his breath for better buoyancy, and this exposes the body of the beast for the kill. The killer closes in, grasps the evil head from behind, and wrenches it away from its meal. Turning the face up towards himself, he plunges his teeth between the bulging eyes, and bites down and in with all his strength. That is the end of it. It dies on the instant.

The writer was asked if he would like to try this method of catching octopus – as the bait. He agreed.

I hope I did not look as yellow as I felt when I stood to take the plunge; I have never been so sick with fear before or since.

I do not suppose it is really true that the eyes of an octopus shine in the dark, besides, it was clear daylight only six feet down in the limpid water; but I could have sworn the brute's eyes burned at me as I turned in towards his cranny. Then I remember chiefly a dreadful sliminess with a herculean power behind it. Something whipped round my left forearm and the back of my neck, binding the two together. In the same flash another something slapped itself high on my forehead, and I felt it crawling down inside the back of my singlet. My impulse was to tear at it with my right hand, but I felt the whole of that arm pinioned to my ribs. A mouth began to nuzzle below my throat, at the junction of the collar-bones. I forgot there was anyone to save me. Yet something still directed me to hold my breath.

I was awakened from my cowardly trance by a quick, strong pull on my shoulders, back from the cranny. The cables around me tightened painfully, but I knew I was adrift from the reef. I gave a kick, rose to the surface, and turned on my back with the brute sticking out of my chest like a tumour. My mouth was smothered by some flabby moving horror. The suckers felt like hot rings pulling at my skin. It was only two seconds, I suppose, from then to the attack of my deliverer, but it seemed like a century of nausea.

My friend came up between me and the reef. He pounced, pulled, bit down, and the thing was over – for everyone but me. At the sudden relaxation of the tentacles, I let out a great breath, sank, and drew in the next under water. It took the united help of both boys to get me, coughing, heaving, and pretending to join in their delighted laughter, back to the reef. I had to submit there to a kind of war-dance round me, in which the dead beast was slung whizzing past my head from one to the other. I had a chance to observe then that it was not by any stretch of fancy a giant, but just plain average. That took the bulge out of my budding self-esteem. I left hurriedly for the cover of the jetty, and was sick.

Arthur Grimble, *A Pattern of Islands*

Questions to think and talk about

1 Why was he sick?
2 The two boys think that this kind of fishing is great fun. Does this mean that they are braver than Arthur Grimble?
3 If you were to do what he did, which part would you dislike most?
4 What is your opinion of this method of catching an animal?
5 What is your opinion of these methods of catching animals?
   fox hunting
   fishing with rod and line
   ferreting
   shooting pheasants

Writing

Arthur Grimble's description of the fight with the octopus is full of action and it is very easy for the reader to imagine just what it was like. Read the story through again and try to see how he achieves this. Now write a description of a struggle or a fight. Either choose your own topic or take one from this list.
   The wrestling match
   The dog fight
   The one that got away
   Quicksands

Crooks who net the big money

The world's protected species – rare wild animals whose export and import are strictly controlled by licence – are the chief target of smugglers.

For that's where the big money lies.

In this country, rare birds, such as hyacinth macaws, sell for £7,000 a pair. Australian golden-shouldered parrots fetch £7,500 a pair.

Exotic zoo animals come even more expensive – £16,000 a pair for gorillas, £9,500 for a single black rhino.

The prices are quoted in mail-order lists sent out by dealers to private collectors, zoo owners, and other dealers.

As soon as word goes round the international grapevine that a new safari park is opening, the offers come pouring in.

The movement of protected animals is limited by international agreement through CITES, the Convention of International Trade in Endangered Species, of which Britain is a member.

Dealers brush aside the convention by claiming that they are offering animals that are 'captive bred' and therefore outside the regulations.

But so many rare animals are advertised that it is impossible for them all to have been captive bred. Yet it is equally impossible to prove they were not.

Questions

1 What is a 'protected species'?
2 Who buys these animals?
3 What international agreement controls this trade?
4 How do the dealers get round it?
5 Why are they not found out?

Agony at the airport and the docks

This falcon has had its eyes sewn up – just to keep it calm.
It was one of a consignment of the birds that arrived at Heathrow from Pakistan. And just another example of the pointless cruelty of the animal trade.

The dealers, knowing the birds would stay quiet if they could not see, used nylon thread and an unsterilized needle to sew the birds' eyelids together. When they arrived in London the birds' eyes were badly infected and it took RSPCA men several hours to remove the stitches.

Neville Whittacker, boss of the Society's airport hostel said: 'The birds suffered agonies. We tried to track down those responsible but it was impossible to prosecute them because it all happened in a foreign country.'

Shipping lines can be as guilty as airlines of making animals suffer.

One case investigated by the highly-respected People's Trust for Endangered Species revealed that four giraffes spent *three months* in crates on board a ship. When they finally staggered out, two of them collapsed and had to be destroyed. The other two recovered.

Most of the blame was put on the British agents who arranged the animals' shipping. For the giraffes were sent from Uganda, via Mombasa to Japan with health certificates for *dogs and cats*.

The Japanese authorities turned them away and the ship went on to Taiwan.

Again they were refused entry. Finally the unfortunate animals were taken to Manila where a home had been found for them.

A trust spokesman said: 'We tried to prosecute but had to abandon the case because we knew it would be torn to shreds in court.'

Questions

6 Why were the falcons' eyes sewn up?
7 Why weren't the people who did it prosecuted?
8 Where did the giraffes begin their journey?
9 Why were they in the crates so long?
10 Why would the Trust's case have been 'torn to shreds in court'?

The moneyspinner

American officials have been put in a spin by the Miami merry-go-round. The scheme hinges on America's reluctance to admit birds from some eastern countries because of the dangers of disease.

British dealers have contacts in America – Miami is a favourite area – who let them know when a consignment of birds has been refused entry. The dealer steps in, buys them at rock bottom prices and flies them back to England.

Here the birds do the required thirty days quarantine and are then flown back. BACK to America – as British-bred birds. There is no problem then about them being admitted. One dealer is reputed to have made £100,000 recently on one merry-go-round.

Daily Mirror 21 November 1979

Question

11 Explain in your own words how these dealers make so much money on the Miami merry-go-round.

Defining a horse

Sissy Dupe is a pupil at school. Her teacher is Mr Gradgrind.

Gradgrind demanded of her: 'Give me your definition of a horse.'

(Sissy Dupe thrown into the greatest alarm by this demand. Found it impossible.)

'Girl number twenty unable to define a horse!' said Mr Gradgrind for the general astonishment of all. 'Girl number twenty possessed of no facts in reference to one of the commonest of animals! Some boys's definition of a horse. Bitzer, yours.'

Bitzer ready. 'Quadruped. Gramnivorous. Forty teeth, namely twenty-four grinders, four eye-teeth, and twelve incisive. Sheds coat in spring. In marshy country, sheds hoofs too. Hoofs hard, but requiring to be shod with iron. Age known by marks in mouth.' Thus Bitzer.

'Now girl number twenty,' said Mr Gradgrind to Sissy, 'you know what a horse is.'

Charles Dickens, *Hard Times*

Hast thou given the horse his might?
Hast thou clothed his neck with the quivering mane?
Hast thou made him to leap as a locust?
The glory of his snorting is terrible.
He paweth in the valley, and rejoiceth in his strength:
He goeth out to meet the armed men . . .

Job chapter 39, verses 19–21: *Revised Standard Version of The Bible*

Horse and Rider by **Titian**, courtesy of the Ashmolean Museum, Oxford.

On being asked to write a school hymn

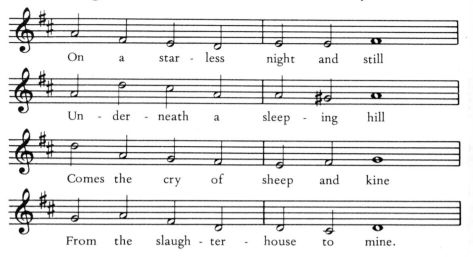

On a star-less night and still

Un-der-neath a sleep-ing hill

Comes the cry of sheep and kine

From the slaugh-ter-house to mine.

Fearful is the call and clear
That I do not want to hear,
Though it has been said by some
That the animal is dumb.

Gone the byre and gone the breeze
And the gently-moving trees
As with stabbing eye they run
In a clear, electric sun.

Now, red-fingered to their trade
With the shot and with the blade,
Rubber-booted angels white
Enter as the morning light.

But who wields that knife and gun
Does not strike the blow alone,
And there is no place to stand
Other than at his right hand.

God, who does not dwell on high
In the wide, unwinking sky,
And whose quiet counsels start
Simply from the human heart.

Teach us strong and teach us true
What to say and what to do,
That we love as best we can
All thy creatures. Even man.

Charles Causley

Bedtime Story

Long long ago when the world was a wild place
Planted with bushes and peopled by apes, our
Mission Brigade was at work in the jungle.
        Hard by the Congo

Once when a foraging detail was active
Scouting for green-fly, it came on a grey man,
   the
Last living man, in the branch of a baobab
        Stalking a monkey.

Earlier men had disposed of, for pleasure,
Creatures whose names we scarcely remember –
Zebra, rhinoceros, elephants, wart-hog,
        Lion, rats, deer. But

After the wars had extinguished the cities
Only the wild ones were left, half-naked
Near the Equator: and here was the last one,
        Starved for a monkey.

By then the Mission Brigade had encountered
Hundreds of such men: and their procedure,
History tells us, was only to feed them:
        Find them and feed them.

Those were the orders. And this was the last one.
Nobody knew that he was, but he was. Mud
Caked on his flat grey flanks. He was crouched,
   half-armed with a shaved spear

Glinting beneath broad leaves. When their jaws
   cut
Swathes through the bark and he saw fine teeth
   shine,
Round eyes roll around and forked arms waver
        Huge as the rough trunks

Over his head, he was frightened. Our workers
Marched through the Congo before he was born,
   but
This was the first time perhaps that he'd seen
   one.
        Staring in hot still

Silence, he crouched there: then jumped. With a
   long swing
Down from his branch, he had angled his spear
   too
Quickly, before they could hold him, and hurled
   it
        Hard at the soldier

Leading the detail. How could he know Queen's
Orders were only to help him? The soldier
Winced when the tipped spear pricked him.
   Unsheathing his
        Sting was a reflex.

Later the Queen was informed. There were no
   more
Men. An impetuous soldier had killed off,
Purely by chance, the penultimate primate.
        When she was certain,

Squadrons of workers were fanned through the
   Congo
Detailed to bring back the man's picked bones to
   be
Sealed in the archives in amber. I'm quite sure
        Nobody found them

After the most industrious search, though.
Where had the bones gone? Over the earth, dear,
Ground by the teeth of the termites, blown by
   the
        Wind, like the dodo's.

George MacBeth

Never cry wolf

Farley Mowat set out to study wolves. He went into the wilds of Canada alone. He pitched his tent and prepared to begin his research.

Quite by accident I had pitched my tent within ten yards of one of the major paths used by the wolves when they were going to, or coming from, their hunting grounds to the westward; and only a few hours after I had taken up residence one of the wolves came back from a trip and discovered me and my tent. He was at the end of a hard night's work and was clearly tired and anxious to go home to bed. He came over a small rise fifty yards from me with his head down, his eyes half-closed, and a preoccupied air about him. Far from being the preternaturally alert and suspicious beast of fiction, this wolf was so self-engrossed that he came straight on to within fifteen yards of me, and might have gone right past the tent without seeing it at all, had I not banged my elbow against the teakettle, making a resounding clank. The wolf's head came up and his eyes opened wide, but he did not stop or falter in his pace. One brief, sidelong glance was all he vouchsafed to me as he continued on his way.

It was true that I wanted to be inconspicuous, but I felt uncomfortable at being so totally ignored. Nevertheless, during the two weeks which followed, one or more wolves used the track past my tent almost every night – and never, except on one memorable occasion, did they evince the slightest interest in me.

By the time this happened I had learned a good deal about my wolfish neighbours, and one of the facts which had emerged was that they were not nomadic roamers, as is almost universally believed, but were settled beasts and the possessors of a large permanent estate with very definite boundaries.

The territory owned by my wolf family comprised more than a hundred square miles, bounded on one side by a river but otherwise not delimited by geographical features. Nevertheless there *were* boundaries, clearly indicated in wolfish fashion.

Anyone who has observed a dog doing his neighbourhood rounds and leaving his personal mark on each convenient post will have already guessed how the wolves marked out *their* property. Once a week, more or less, the clan made the rounds of the family lands and freshened up the boundary markers – a sort of lupine beating of the bounds. This careful attention to property rights was perhaps made necessary by the presence of two other wolf families whose lands abutted on ours, although I never discovered any evidence of bickering or disagreements between the owners of the various adjoining estates. I suspect, therefore, that it was more of a ritual activity.

In any event, once I had become aware of the strong feeling of property rights which existed amongst the wolves, I decided to use this knowledge to make them at least recognize my existence. One evening, after they had gone off for their regular nightly hunt, I staked out a property claim of my own, embracing perhaps three acres, with the tent at the middle, and *including a hundred-yard long section of the wolves' path*.

Staking the land turned out to be rather more difficult than I had anticipated. In order to ensure that my claim would not be overlooked, I felt obliged to make a property mark on stones, clumps of moss, and patches of vegetation at intervals of not more than fifteen feet around the circumference of my claim. This took most of the night and required frequent returns to the tent to consume copious quantities of tea; but before dawn brought the

hunters home the task was done, and I retired, somewhat exhausted, to observe results.

I had not long to wait. At 0814 hours, according to my wolf log, the leading male of the clan appeared over the ridge behind me, padding homeward with his usual air of preoccupation. As usual he did not deign to glance at the tent; but when he reached the point where my property line intersected the trail, he stopped as abruptly as if he had run into an invisible wall. He was only fifty yards from me and with my binoculars I could see his expression very clearly.

His attitude of fatigue vanished and was replaced by a look of bewilderment. Cautiously he extended his nose and sniffed at one of my marked bushes. He did not seem to know what to make of it or what to do about it. After a minute of complete indecision he backed away a few yards and sat down. And then, finally, he looked directly at the tent and at me. It was a long, thoughtful, considering sort of look.

Having achieved my object – that of forcing at least one of the wolves to take cognizance of my existence – I now began to wonder if, in my ignorance, I had transgressed some unknown wolf law of major importance and would have to pay for my temerity. I found myself regretting the absence of a weapon as the look I was getting became longer, yet more thoughtful, and still more intent.

I began to grow decidedly fidgety, for I dislike staring matches, and in this particular case I was up against a master, whose yellow glare seemed to become more baleful as I attempted to stare him down.

The situation was becoming intolerable. In an effort to break the impasse I loudly cleared my throat and turned my back on the wolf (for a tenth of a second) to indicate as clearly as possible that I found his continued scrutiny impolite, if not actually offensive.

He appeared to take the hint. Getting to his feet he had another sniff at my marker, and then he seemed to make up his mind. Briskly, and with an air of decision, he turned his attention away from me and began a systematic tour of the area I had staked out as my own. As he came to each boundary marker he sniffed it once or twice, then carefully placed *his* mark on the outside of each clump of grass or stone. As I watched I saw where I, in my ignorance, had erred. He made his mark with such economy that he was able to complete the entire circuit without having to reload once, or, to change the simile slightly, he did it all on one tank of fuel.

The task completed – and it had taken him no longer than fifteen minutes – he rejoined the path at the point where it left my property and trotted off towards his home – leaving me with a good deal to occupy my thoughts.

Farley Mowat, *Never Cry Wolf*

Puzzles

Which animal?

In each of these rhymes by Ogden Nash the name of the creature he is describing has been left out: you have to work out what it is. To make things a little more difficult the verse has been printed as if it was ordinary sentences, and no blank has been left where the name should be.

1   The song of never varies, and when they're moulting they're pretty revolting.
2   How many Scientists have written the is gentle as a kitten! Yet this I know about the: his bite is worser than his bark.
3   Myself, I rather like the, it's not a mouse, it's not a rat. It has no feathers, yet has wings, it's quite inaudible when it sings. It zigzags through the evening air and never lands on ladies' hair, a fact of which men spend their lives attempting to convince their wives.

Word study

All these words appear in this unit. The number after each one tells you which page it is on.

consignment   136   foraging   141
reputed   137   reflex   141
quadruped   138   resounding   142
kine   140   copious   143
counsels   140   scrutiny   144

1   Find each word and read the sentence it is in.
2   Write each word on a new line, and against it write what you think it means. If you don't know, have a guess.
3   When you have done all of them, look them up in the dictionary.
4   Write the correct meanings of any that you got wrong.

Watching wild mammals

In this passage every seventh word has been missed out. Read it through and try to work out what the words should be. Then write the number of each blank and the word you think should go there.

A family of keen-eyed naturalists ....¹.... for a walk will usually see ....².... of birds around them, but they ....³.... not see many mammals – perhaps a ....⁴.... squirrels chasing through the trees, the ....⁵.... hare loping across a field, and ....⁶.... a fleeting glimpse of a deer, ...⁷.... rarely anything more. This is because ....⁸.... of our mammals are timid and ....⁹.... creatures and the majority come out ....¹⁰.... at night. Special techniques are therefore ....¹¹.... if you want to watch mammals, ...¹².... if a few simple rules are ....¹³.... you will find that even a ....¹⁴.... garden or back yard may contain ....¹⁵.... interesting species. Hedgerows and woodlands contain ....¹⁶.... more.

    Watching by night is obviously ....¹⁷.... to be more productive than watching ....¹⁸.... day, but it is necessary to ....¹⁹.... a certain amount of 'homework' if ....²⁰.... want to have a reasonable chance ....²¹.... success. First of all, you must ....²².... that there are animals of the ....²³.... that you want to watch living ....²⁴.... your area, and you must find ....²⁵.... more or less where they are ....²⁶.... . You can do this by looking ....²⁷.... burrows, tracks and various other signs. ....²⁸.... you can make a careful survey ....²⁹.... the area to decide the most ....³⁰.... viewpoint. This survey is especially important ....³¹.... you are going out at night, ...³².... it enables you to note the ....³³.... of fallen branches, potholes, and other ....³⁴.... which might not be so obvious ....³⁵.... the dark. You will then be ....³⁶.... to pick your way carefully round ....³⁷.... without hurting yourself and without disturbing ....³⁸.... animals when you go back at ....³⁹.... . Ideally, you should select at least ....⁴⁰.... , because mammals have very ....⁴¹.... noses and they will smell you ....⁴².... easily if you are upwind of ....⁴³.... : with two sites to choose from ....⁴⁴.... do have a chance to get ....⁴⁵.... of the animals. You should also ....⁴⁶.... hidden from the animals as much ....⁴⁷.... possible, and you should avoid creating ....⁴⁸.... shadow with your body. The ideal ....⁴⁹.... is sitting with your back against ....⁵⁰.... tree or a rock for support, ...⁵¹.... this is not always possible and ....⁵².... may well have to put up ....⁵³.... some discomfort if you want to ....⁵⁴.... the animals for long.

Michael Chinery, *The Family Naturalist*

SCHOOL 2025

What will schools be like in the year 2025? What do you think they *should* be like?

In this unit you are asked to design your own school for the year 2025. Each section takes a different aspect of school life. It shows you how it has changed over the years. Then there are questions to think and talk about, writing, and research topics.

Questions to think and talk about

1 What are the biggest changes that have taken place in schools over the last thirty years?
2 What changes do you think will happen in the next thirty years?
3 What are the most important things that *need* changing?

Buildings

School 1870

School 1970

School 2025?

The boarding school stood on land enclosed by a bend in the River Thames. The main part, including the games area and most of the classrooms, was in late twentieth-century style, bare and sprawling. The boarding houses which marched along the inner perimeter were more recent, austere within but their exteriors coloured and ornamented. Rob had been allotted to G-House, which was pastel blue crossed by broad transverse stripes of orange.

For the first few days he was too confused to take in much beyond an impression of constant activity. The day was filled to overflowing. Broadcast alarms woke the dormitories at six-thirty and there was a scramble to reach the games area by seven. They were nearly a quarter of a mile from it – only H-House was farther off . . .

. . . There was no library in the school, no books except those used as aids to the various visual learning techniques. He had not really thought there would be, but it was a blow all the same . . .

John Christopher, *The Guardians*

Questions to think and talk about	1 What are the main differences you can see between the two pictures?
	2 Why do you think school buildings changed in this way?
	3 What would the 1870s school have been like for the children?
	4 What would it be like to be a pupil at the school John Christopher describes?
	5 How does your school and its buildings compare with these three schools?
	6 What do you think school buildings will be like in 2025?
Writing	Design a school for the year 2025. Either make a drawing of it, or draw a plan. In either case use labels to show the different parts of the school. Write a description of what it will be like.
Research	Look at the school buildings in your district. Try to find out the answers to these questions:

1 When was each one built?
2 Which is the oldest building?
3 Which is the oldest site? (A new school is often built on the site of an older school.)
4 Which is the best designed?

Classrooms and uniforms

A 19th century classroom

Our dress was of the coarsest and quaintest kind, but was respected out of doors and is still so. It consisted of a blue drugget gown, or body, with ample skirts to it; a yellow vest underneath in winter-time; small-clothes of Russia duck; worsted yellow stockings; a leathern girdle; and a little black worsted cap, usually carried in the hand. I believe it was the ordinary dress of children in humble life during the reign of the Tudors.

Leigh Hunt, *Autobiography*

19th-century uniform

A 1970s' classroom

Questions to think and talk about

1 How do the classrooms in your school compare with those in the pictures?
2 What would lessons have been like in the 19th century classroom?
3 How would they be different in the 20th century classroom?
4 Why do schools have uniforms?
5 The 19th century uniform may seem strange, but it is in fact still worn in a similar form by the pupils at Christ's Hospital School. How would the clothes you wear at school look to someone in 2025?
6 What will school uniform be like in 2025?

Writing

1 Design a classroom for the year 2025. Draw a labelled plan of it and write a short explanation.
2 Design a school uniform for 2025. Make a drawing and write an explanation.

Learning

A Victorian primary school

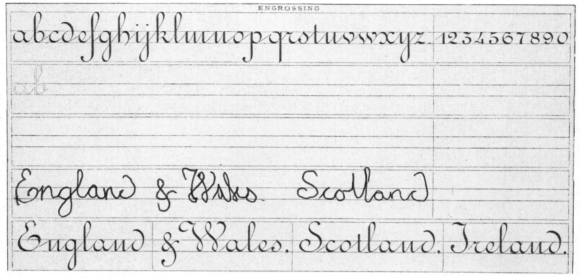

Reading, writing, and arithmetic were the principal subjects, with a Scripture lesson every morning, and needlework every afternoon for girls.

Every morning at ten o'clock the Rector arrived to take the older children for Scripture. His lesson consisted of Bible reading, turn and turn about round the class, of reciting from memory the names of the kings of Israel and repeating the Church Catechism. After that he would deliver a little lecture on morals and behaviour. The children must not lie or steal or be discontented or envious.

Arithmetic was considered the most important of the subjects taught, and those who were good at figures ranked high in their classes. It was very simple arithmetic, extending only to the first four rules, with the money sums, known as 'bills of parcels', for the most advanced pupils.

The writing lesson consisted of the copying of copperplate maxims: 'A fool and his money are soon parted'; 'Waste not, want not'; 'Count ten before you speak', and so on. Once a week composition would be set, usually in the form of writing a letter describing some recent event. This was regarded chiefly as a spelling test.

Flora Thompson, *Lark Rise to Candleford*

School activities in the 1970s

Questions to think and talk about	1	People are no longer taught copperplate writing; handwriting has probably become much less neat and tidy. Does it matter?

Questions to think and talk about

1 People are no longer taught copperplate writing; handwriting has probably become much less neat and tidy. Does it matter?
2 What are the 'principal subjects' in your timetable?
3 What will the 'principal subjects' be in 2025?
4 Since Flora Thompson's schooldays great scientific progress has been made. Which of these inventions do you think has changed schools most:

radio
sound recording
TV
video recording
satellite communications
the microcomputer

5 How will scientific discoveries and inventions affect schools in 2025?

Writing

1 Make a list of the subjects that will be taught in your school of 2025. Work out how much time will be given to each subject each week.
2 Write a day's timetable for a class like yours in 2025. For each lesson write a short description of what happens in it.

Teachers and discipline

A Victorian village schoolmistress

She was a bunched and punitive little body and the school had christened her Crabby; she had a sour yellow look, lank hair coiled in earphones, and the skin and voice of a turkey. We were all afraid of the gobbling Miss B; she spied, she pried, she crouched, she crept, she pounced – she was a terror.

Each morning was war without declaration; no one knew who would catch it next. We stood to attention, half-crippled in our desks, till Miss B walked in, whacked the walls with a ruler and fixed us with her squinting eye. 'Good a-morning, children!' 'Good morning, Teacher!' The greeting was like a rattling of swords. Then she would scowl at the floor and begin to growl 'Ar Farther . . .'; at which we said the Lord's Prayer, praised all good things, and thanked God for the health of our King. But scarcely had we bellowed the last Amen than Crabby coiled, uncoiled and sprang, and knocked some poor boy sideways.

One seldom knew why; one was always off guard, for the punishment preceded the charge. The charge, however, followed hard upon it, to a light shower of angry spitting.

'Shuffling your feet! Playing with the desk! A-smirking at that miserable Betty! I will not have it. I'll not, I say. I repeat – I will not have it!'

Laurie Lee, *Cider With Rosie*

Summerhill

Summerhill is an experimental school. It was founded in 1921 by A. S. Neill who believed in total freedom for his pupils.

Lessons in Summerhill are optional. Children can go to them or stay away from them – for years if they want to. There is a timetable for the staff, and the children have classes according to their age usually, but sometimes according to their interests. Personally I do not know what type of teaching is carried on, for I never visit lessons, and have no interest in how children learn. We have no new methods of teaching because we do not consider that teaching very much matters. Whether a school has an apparatus for teaching Long Division is of no importance whatever.

Children who come as infants attend lessons all the way, but pupils from other schools vow that they will never attend any beastly lessons again. They play and cycle and get in people's way, but they fight shy of any lessons. This sometimes goes on for months, and the recovery time is proportionate to the hatred their last school gave them. Our record case was a girl from a convent. She loafed for three years. The average period of recovery from lesson-aversion is three months.

A. S. Neill, *That Dreadful School*

Questions to think and talk about	1 Do teachers have to be strict? 2 What would happen if they were never strict? 3 Would you like to attend a school like Summerhill? 4 In your school of 2025 what would you do about discipline? 5 How will the teacher's job have changed by 2025? 6 Will it be easier or harder?
Writing	1 Advertise for a new teacher for your 2025 school. Decide what his job will be and the qualities he will need to do it well. Decide how you will advertise: in a newspaper, on radio, or TV? Write your advertisement. 2 Your new teacher starts work. After the first day he goes home and tells his wife about it. Write their conversation as a script.

School report

```
25 JULY 2025

Harwood, Gareth

12 years 10 months

form: 2Y3

subject grades:

Astrophysics: B-

Computing: C+

Language arts: B+

Life Sciences: C

Robotics: C

Space Dynamics: B-

Subject comments:
```

Questions to think and talk about

1 What do these subject titles mean?
2 Are they likely to appear on a 2025 school report form?
3 What subjects do you think will appear on reports in 2025?

Writing Write the subject comments for Gareth Harwood's report.

Section B: Skills

Contents

Parts of speech

Nouns Nouns are words we use to name **people** : man, professor
                                               places : garage, hill
                                               things : stone, telescope
                                               ideas : peace, terror

In this passage, all the *nouns* have been printed in *italics*.

I opened the *door* very quietly and walked into the *room*. It was dark and quiet. My *eyes* got used to the *darkness* and I saw in the *corner* a large wooden *box*.

Adjectives We use adjectives to qualify nouns. 'Qualify' means 'say more about'. In this passage, all the **adjectives** are in **bold** type.

The gun looked **large** and **dangerous**. I picked it up carefully in my **right** hand. Its **grey** barrel looked very **sinister** in the **bright** moonlight.

Verbs Verbs are words we use to describe **actions** : run, hit
                                                  states : seem, appear
                                                  changes : become, grow
There are also auxiliary verbs. These work with other verbs. The main ones are:

be   am   is   are   was   were   being   been
has   have   had   having
may   might   can   could   must   ought
will   shall   would   should   do   did

In this passage all the *verbs* (including *auxiliaries*) are in *italics*.

Friday *was* a bad day. I *got* out of bed and *put* my foot right in a cup of tea my mother *had left* for me. Things *would* not *have been* too bad, if I *had* not *tripped* on the top stair as I *was going* down to breakfast.

Adverbs Adverbs modify verbs, adjectives or other adverbs. 'Modify' means 'say more about'. In this paragraph the **adverbs** are in **bold** type.

Jason peered **guiltily** round the door. He had **just** broken his father's new camera. He had picked it up **excitedly**, pretended to take a couple of action photographs, and he had dropped it. He had picked it up **extremely carefully** but he knew **immediately** that it was broken.

Exercises

A **Make a list of all the nouns in this passage. Include all proper nouns (the names of people or places).**

A man was walking from Hereford to Cardiff. After some time he felt very tired and began to wonder how many miles he still had to go. Then he met a farmer going in the opposite direction.

'How far is it to Cardiff?' asked the traveller.

'With a cow, or without a cow?' said the farmer.

'Without a cow, of course,' answered the traveller.

'I don't know,' said the farmer. 'I've never done it without a cow.'

B **Make a list of all the adjectives in this passage.**

A man rushed up to a policeman.

'I've lost my wife!' he said. 'Can you find her for me?'

'First you must describe her,' said the policeman. 'How tall was she?'

'I . . . er . . . don't know.'

'Was her hair light or dark?'

'I don't know.'

'Was she slim or stout?'

'I don't know, but she took the dog with her.'

'What kind of dog was it?'

'A black and white spaniel with one brown ear. It had one leg shorter than the others and walked with a slight limp. There was a small scar above the right eye and the left ear was two centimetres longer than the right ear.'

'I can't help you about your wife,' said the policeman, 'but we'll find the dog for you!'

C **Make a list of all the verbs in this passage. In each case, make sure that you write down the whole verb.**

A boy left school and started work as a builder's labourer. One day he thought, 'My hair is getting too long.' So he decided to go to the barber's. Just as he was leaving the site he met the foreman.

'Where are you going?' asked the foreman.

'To the barber's,' said the boy.

'Oh no you are not. Not in my time.'

'Why not?' asked the boy. 'After all my hair grew in your time – so it should be cut in your time!'

Sentences

Types of sentence

There are three types of sentence:

Statement : Mary is at home.
Question : Where is Mary?
Command : Go home!

Parts of a sentence

Sentences normally have a subject and a verb.

Subject	Verb	Rest of the sentence
Mary Who	is did	at home. that?

In commands the subject is you. It is usually left out.

(You)	Go	home!

Number

The subject of a sentence can be singular or plural. Some verbs change according to whether the subject is singular or plural.

Singular : He is champion of the world.
Plural : They are not as good as John.

Further examples

In these examples the *subject* is in *italics* and the **verb** is in **bold type**.

STATEMENTS
singular subject : *The longest earthworm ever* **was** over a metre long.
plural subject : *Earthworms* **improve** the soil.

QUESTIONS
singular : When **did** *Uncle Arbuthnot* **visit** Pompeii?
plural : *Who* **are** those girls with green hair?

COMMANDS
singular : **Wash** your face at once!
plural : **Wash** your faces at once!

Exercises

A **Are these sentences statements, questions or commands?**

1 Just leave me alone.
2 Is Doreen really leaving school?
3 How do you know?
4 I should like to know why they did that.
5 People in glass houses should not throw stones.
6 Don't be silly!
7 Where are you going now?
8 Does Halloween come before or after Guy Fawkes Day?
9 In Scotland New Year's Eve is called Hogmanay.
10 Leave off!

B **Write down the subject of each of these sentences.**

1 Peter and his grandfather went to see Liverpool play last night.
2 Several of the girls in our class are absent today.
3 Walking along the road, the blind man was guided by his dog.
4 Even in December Ginnie does not wear a coat to school.
5 After Peter and Suzanne, I had my go on the big swing.

Write down the verb in each of these sentences.

6 They all enjoyed the game very much.
7 You will never see a kipper swimming around.
8 It would have been fun to visit Madame Tussaud's.
9 Even yesterday Dave wanted to stay at home and read.
10 The ancient Romans seem to have been very warlike.

C **For each of these sentences write down the correct word to fill the space. Choose your answer from the brackets at the end of the sentence.**

1 Either my father or my mother always ___ with me to buy clothes. (come/comes)
2 All the class, including Jane, ___ to go to London for the summer trip. (want/wants)
3 The strongest of the boys ___ Brett. (is/are)
4 The strongest of the boys ___ Brett and Martin. (was/were)
5 Peter is better than me at swimming and I ___ better than him at athletics. (is/am/are)
6 There ___ three girls in our class called Mary but only one of them ___ glasses. (is/are, wear/wears)
7 My sister and I ___ always having rows. (is/am/are)
8 Ice cream and strawberry jam ___ well together. (go/goes)
9 Either ice cream or strawberry jam ___ a good way to finish off your tea. (is/are)

More about adjectives

In a sentence, an adjective can be a single word,
or a phrase,
or a clause.

Single word   In these sentences, the adjectives are in **bold type**.

1   Our house has a **green** door.
2   Mary is a **pretty** girl.

Phrase   A phrase is a group of words. In these sentences the adjective phrases are in **bold type**.

1   Our house has a door **with green paint on it**.
2   Mary is a girl with **long blonde hair**.

Clause   If a phrase contains a complete verb it is called a clause. In these sentences the adjective clauses are in **bold type**.

1   Our house has a door **that Dad painted green**.
2   Mary is a girl **whose hair is long and blonde**.

Summary   The same job can be done by a single word, a phrase or a clause.

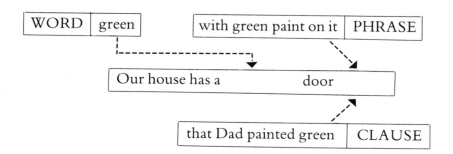

Exercises

A   Rewrite each of these sentences. Replace the adjective in bold type with a phrase or clause.

1   I feel sure that I know that **tall** man.
2   Jimmy likes playing **team** games.
3   I met David on a **fine** day.
4   Please pass me the **red** book.
5   Did you see that **peculiar** programme on TV?
6   I don't like **sticky** cakes.
7   He was an **unusual** person.
8   They live in a **large** house.
9   We had an **exciting** holiday.
10   She had an **ugly** face.

B   In each of these sentences a phrase or clause is in bold type. Rewrite the sentence and replace these words with one word.

Example : I like reading books **that are full of excitement and adventure.**
Answer   : I like reading exciting books.

1   We went for a walk **of over twelve miles.**
2   She made a cake **that contained raisins and sultanas.**
3   In woodwork we made stools **of beech and pine.**
4   The scientist sometimes has to do experiments **which can have dangerous results.**
5   Our team plays football in a way **that produces goals.**
6   She bought a set of hair curlers **that work by electricity.**
7   He got a school report **with a lot of bad comments on it.**
8   For his birthday he was given a bike **with drop handlebars and ten speeds.**
9   Near the house there is a hill **over a thousand feet high.**
10   Sarah's room is always full of things **scattered everywhere.**

C   Look at the sentences in Exercise B. In each case decide whether the words in bold type form a phrase or a clause. Write down 'clause' or 'phrase' for each.

D   For each of the words in this list:
   i   write a phrase or clause that has a similar meaning.
   ii   write a sentence containing your phrase or clause.

Example : big
Answer   : weighing twenty stone
             On the bus I saw a man weighing twenty stone.

1	small	3	happy	5	poor	7	talkative
2	sad	4	strange	6	quiet	8	busy

Pronouns

Pronouns are words that are used to stand instead of nouns. They save us having to repeat a noun.

Example
The hunter tracked the lion and then the hunter shot the lion.
becomes
The hunter tracked the lion and then **he** shot **it**.

Personal pronouns

I	we	he	she	they
me	us	him	her	them

Impersonal pronouns

it they
    them

Possessive pronouns

my our his her their its your

Guidelines
Try to avoid repeating nouns and names. Use pronouns instead.
But, do not use a pronoun unless it is clear which noun it refers to.

Relative pronouns

A clause that replaces an adjective (see page 162) is called a relative clause. Relative clauses are usually introduced by relative pronouns:
who   which   that
whom
whose

Examples

The man	who	spoke to you	is my teacher.
The girl	whom	you nearly knocked down	is very cross.
The person	whose	wallet you found	is very pleased.
The bus	which	is just leaving	is the last one tonight.
The bike	that	you are riding	is mine.

relative   relative
pronouns   clauses

Exercises   **A**   **Rewrite these sentences. Replace any nouns or names that are repeated with suitable pronouns.**

1 Jayne told me that Jayne is going to Spain on holiday.
2 I found a book and I put the book on your table.
3 John and Katherine had a row because John said that Katherine had taken John's pen and put the pen in Katherine's desk.
4 Passengers are reminded that passengers should not put passengers' heads out of the window.
5 I think that you should read this book because I think this book is very interesting.
6 In maths Mr Donaldson told David to do a long-division sum and Mr Donaldson was very cross when David could not do the long-division sum.
7 The Parents' Association has recently been raising money for a new minibus and so far the Parents' Association has collected £500 towards the new minibus.
8 The teacher asked Yvonne why Yvonne had not done the work the teacher told Yvonne to do.
9 Our school has just bought a computer and the computer will be used to work out the timetable.
10 Jeff kicked the ball so hard that the ball went into the bushes and Jeff had to go and look for the ball.

B   **Join each of these pairs of sentences into one sentence by using a relative pronoun.**

1 I have just finished reading a book.
   John lent me the book.
2 Do you know that boy?
   Peter has just spoken to him.
3 What did you do with the tennis racket?
   I lent you the tennis racket last week.
4 I have just had a letter from Mary.
   Mary's family moved to Edinburgh last year.
5 I have lost a very important piece of paper.
   I had written on it the answers to my maths homework.
6 What is the name of that girl over there.
   She came to the school last term.
7 My mother has just mended my jacket.
   I tore my jacket last week.
8 Today I saw that boy called Higgins.
   His arm was broken in a game of football.
9 I caught that guinea pig.
   The guinea pig escaped last week.
10 I'm going to London with Jackie.
   Jackie's older brother is a disc jockey.

Writing letters to people you know

Setting out a letter

27 Elm Park
Hornchurch
Essex
RM21 3P2

1 Your address

Tuesday, 14th February 1982

2 The date

Dear Mr Bateson,

3 The greeting

    I have tried to get in touch with you several times about the noise your children make, but I have had no success.

4 The letter

    Every night between 7 and 10 o'clock they play pop music very loud. The wall between our houses is very thin so the music is very disturbing. I feel I have the right to some peace in the evenings.

    Please tell your children to make less noise or I shall have to complain to the Council.

Yours sincerely,

A T Frerm

5 The closing phrase

6 Your signature

Addressing the envelope

Mr J. Bateson
25 Elm Park
HORNCHURCH
Essex
RM21 3P2

1 The person's title and name
2 Number and street
3 Post town in capitals
4 County
5 Postcode in capitals

Greetings and closing phrases

The most widely-used ones are:

1   To people you do not know at all: *Dear Sir,*
                                                    Yours faithfully,

2   To people you know a little: *Dear Mr/Mrs/Miss/Ms........,*
                                                  Yours sincerely,

With *Yours faithfully*, you normally sign with your initials and surname. You usually do this with *Yours sincerely* as well, unless you are 'on Christian name terms' with the person you are writing to. In that case you sign with your first name and your surname. Remember that the words *sincerely* and *faithfully* always begin with a small letter when used in a closing phrase.

Exercises

A   Write an answer to the letter on page 166.

B   Write an answer to this letter:

> 1793 Bay Boulevard
> Montville
> California
> U.S.A.
>
> 15th October   1981
>
> Dear Janet Graves,
>
>   Last month I was on holiday in Britain. I met your Uncle Charles in London and during our many conversations he told me all about you and your family.
>   I am doing the research for a book about British schools. I should like to include information about how school pupils feel about their schools. In particular I should like to know their opinions about how their schools are organised, how they are taught and what changes they would like to see made.
>   If you could find the time to write me along these lines, I should be most interested and grateful.
>
>   Yours sincerely,
>   *K.A.Mare*.
>   K.A. LeMare

Writing business letters

Business letters are usually sent to (or from) offices in which a number of people work. Normally the writer does not know the person he is writing to. Because of this, business letters are set out differently from other letters. There are many different styles, but the one on this page is most suitable for handwritten business letters.

92 Norewood Lane
Ilford
Essex
IL2 4DJ

1 Your address

2 The title and address of the person you are writing to

The Mayor
Town Hall
Bognor Regis
Sussex   2nd September 1982

3 The date

4 The greeting (usually 'Dear Sir,')

Dear Sir,

5 The first paragraph always says what the letter is about.

I wish to complain about your advertisements in the Sunday Express and other newspapers.

In these advertisements it says, 'Come to Sunny Bognor for a Fun-filled Holiday'. I have just spent two weeks in your town. It poured with rain all the time and it certainly was not fun.

I think you should stop this misleading advertising at once. I demand my money back.

6 The closing phrase (usually 'Yours faithfully,')

Yours faithfully,

7 Your signature (initials and surname)

T. Hopkins

169

A **Write an answer to the letter on page 168.**

B **You have seen one of these advertisements in the paper. Write a letter asking for more information.**

Skan Adventure Holidays

Are you between the ages of 10 and 15? If so, Skan is for you. We offer exciting adventure holidays for *every* taste. Write for free colour brochure to:

Skan Adventure Holidays,
P.O. Box 65,
Green Lane,
Birmingham.

THE BLEEPER!

A fantastic two-way radio system that doubles as a burglar alarm. Only £9.95 fully guaranteed.

Write for further details to:

D.O.D.G.Y. Electronics,
Widemarsh Street,
Hertford,
SG8 6YB

C **Write an answer to this letter:**

Miss V. Patch
Waterworks Road
Corby
Northants

Personal Charm Ltd
Nirvana Street
Manchester

13th December 1983

Dear Madam,

    Your name has been recommended to us by a friend as being someone who has a sure eye for the latest fashions.

    As you probably know, we market a wide range of cosmetics for the older lady. We feel sure that when you see our latest range you will want to become a representative straight away. We have sent the £35 sample package by rail and it will be with you any day now. Full instructions about selling the cosmetics and how to pay us are included.

    We hope you enjoy selling our products.

Yours faithully,

J. Grundy, Sales Manager

Sentences, capital letters, and full stops

Sentences Every sentence must be separated from other sentences. This is done by punctuation.

Begin every sentence with a capital letter and end it with a full stop.

Capital letters Capital letters are also used for these things:

1	The word 'I':	I
2	Names:	James Witherspoon
		Coca Cola
3	The main words in titles:	Department of the Environment
		My Family and Other Animals
4	For days and months:	Monday
		December
5	For initials:	J. J. Witherspoon
		BBC

Full stops Full stops are also used for these things:

1	After initials:	J. J. Witherspoon
		N.E.D.C.
2	After some abbreviations:	Sun. for Sunday
		Yorks. for Yorkshire

Exceptions These are often written without full stops:

1 The initials of very well-known organisations:
BBC   UNESCO   FBA
2 These titles: Mr   Mrs   Ms   Dr   Revd   Mme   Mlle

Using abbreviations In formal writing, abbreviations are not normally used. Write out names and titles in full. There are some exceptions to this:
personal titles, like Mr and Dr
initials of very well-known organisations, like BBC

Exercises

A **Write out these sentences putting in full stops and capital letters where needed.**

1 in our area we get atv programmes and bbc midlands
2 yesterday was peter's birthday and i gave him a biggles book by w e johns
3 our english teacher is miss davidson
4 i have just finished reading a book about american sports cars by eric proust
5 my mother helps with the meals on wheels service run by the wrvs
6 on tuesdays my brother pete goes to scouts and on thursdays i watch hillesley f c
7 the letters unesco stand for united nations educational scientific and cultural organisation
8 it always rains on august bank holiday
9 when our car broke down on the m6 near preston my dad wished he had joined the aa
10 last summer we went by br to dover, by sealink to calais, and by sncf to paris

B **Write out this paragraph, putting in capital letters and full stops where needed.**

february 10th

i am in disgrace i broke the classroom window it was an accident but nobody believed me i threw one of my football boots over my head because i dont like football and the window was in the way miss storey said i shouldn't have had them in the classroom and said, 'Can't you even say sorry?' and when i said, 'It was an accident,' which it was, she was very cross i had to go and see the headmaster and the headmaster sent a note to my parents my father said, 'You are a degenerate. What you need is a psychiatrist!'

Rachel Billington, *Sammy's Diary*

C **Write down the abbreviations for each of the following:**

1 Amateur Athletic Association
2 Doctor of Philosophy
3 Estimated time of arrival
4 Member of Parliament
5 National Society for the Prevention of Cruelty to Children
6 Youth Hostels Association
7 Fellow of the Royal Geographical Association
8 Trades Union Congress
9 Intelligence Quotient
10 Military Cross

Commas and colons

Commas **1** Commas are used to separate the different things in a list.

My interests are: walking, road-racing, reading, and swimming.

2 Commas are used to mark off the first part of the sentence and separate it from the rest.

When the children had finished eating, the headmaster made an announcement.

3 Commas are used to mark off the middle part of a sentence and separate it from the rest.

I saw Peter James, the boy you kicked, in the street.

4 Commas are used to mark off the last part of a sentence and separate it from the rest.

John is coming with us tomorrow, I hope.

5 Commas are used in direct speech – see page 178.

Colons **1** A colon is used to introduce a list.

My interests are: walking, road-racing, reading, and swimming.

Beside him in the boat were found some strange objects: a Bible, a revolver, and three unopened letters.

2 A colon is used to introduce a saying, a statement, or an idea.

He had one great belief: that a man should always tell the truth.
The law says: drive on the left.

3 A colon is used when a sentence contains a contrast.

He supports Spurs: I am an Arsenal fan.
Some people are good at maths: others can't add two and two.

Exercises

A   Punctuate these sentences correctly.

1   there was a saying my mother always used fear god and shame the devil

2   when i emptied my pockets i found three bus tickets a broken pencil a piece of string and some chewing gum

3   after the clock had finished striking our english teacher told us to stop writing

4   we are looking for several things old clothes saucepans electrical goods and other secondhand objects

5   sharon clutterbuck who started at our school last week comes from cleethorpes

6   beccles where we spent our holiday last august is on the norfolk broads

7   the school rules are very clear about this pupils must not run in the corridor

8   unless you have got anything else to say i will put my point of view

9   smoking is an unpleasant habit or so i have always believed

10   Eastbourne has everything sunshine clean beaches and lots of entertainments

B   Punctuate this passage correctly.

i was all alone at home that night my parents had gone to a meeting in the town i had finished my homework english and maths then i had switched on the tv and was watching a cowboy film it was not very interesting so i was not giving it my full attention suddenly i realised that there was someone outside the house i heard several clear noises in the garden my heart began to beat faster i was all alone in the house and there was someone wandering around in the garden what should i do i listened intently there it was again there was someone right by the window i froze in terror i was unable to do anything to my horror i heard a sound as if someone was scratching on the window i almost died of fear then slowly the window swung open and in walked our cat

C   Punctuate this passage correctly.

on the night of september 27th ad 1066 a fleet of ships set sail from france to cross the english channel the ships were loaded with about 5000 warriors and their horses arms and supplies a lantern burned brightly at the mast of the flagship which carried william duke of normandy the leader of the expedition his aim was to defeat the english king harold and win the crown of england for himself

Patrick Roke, *The Normans*

Apostrophes

Omission   Apostrophes are used to show where one or more letters have been omitted, or missed out; for example:

we have	becomes	**we've**
who is	becomes	**who's**
are not	becomes	**aren't**
they are	becomes	**they're**
Dad will	becomes	**Dad'll**
you are	becomes	**you're**
I would	becomes	**I'd**
she might have	becomes	**she might've**

Possession   Apostrophes are used to show possession – to show that something belongs to someone.

1   We add **'s** to words that do not end in s.

Jane's bike   **Gran's** house

the **man's** foot   **people's** problems

2   We add just **'** to words that do end in s.

the **girls'** mother   **Charles'** idea

James' friend   **animals'** homes

Exceptions: its (meaning belonging to it)

his

hers

yours

ours

theirs

Exercises

A **Write out these short forms and put in apostrophes where needed.**

theyve   theyre
weve   were
havent   wont
Im   hes
Toms   shouldnt

B **Write out the short forms of the following phrases. Put in apostrophes where needed.**

he will   he will not
I am   I am not
they have   they have not
she is   she is not
we are   we are not
you had   you had not.

C **Write out these sentences and put in the correct form of the words in brackets.**

1   I want to know .... (whose/who's) going to teach us English next term.
2   Dave says .... (theirs/there's/theres) going to be a disco next week.
3   Peter claims that .... (its/it's) his book, but Mary says ....
    .... (its/it's) .... (hers/her's).
4   Yesterday I saw Mary, ... (whose/who's) father has just bought a new car.
5   Sandra and Yvonne say .... (their/there/they're) are a lot of new boys in 2B.
6   .... (They're/there/their) going to Jersey for their holiday.
7   The school has to congratulate .... (its/it's) football team on winning the league.
8   My brother goes to .... (St James/St Jame's/St James') primary school.

Script

Script is the way in which conversations are written down in plays.

1   The names of the speakers are written in capital letters.
2   The names are put underneath each other.
3   A colon (:) is put after the name of each speaker.
4   Only the words the speaker actually says are written down.
5   Each new line of speech starts underneath the one before.

MIKE: Excuse me . . .
DRIVER: Yeah?
MIKE: Could you give me a lift?
DRIVER: Where to?
MIKE: How far are you going?
DRIVER: Warrington.
MIKE: That'll do. That'll do fine.

Instructions

You can also write instructions and explanations for the actors in the play. These instructions and explanations are put in brackets and underlined. This is to show that they are not words the actors speak.

Radio and tape-recorded plays

In radio plays you cannot see the actors, so there isn't much point in telling them what actions to do. On the other hand, *how* they speak is very important. The directions are written between brackets and underlined.

MIKE: (Anxiously.) Excuse me...
DRIVER: (Bored.) Yeah?

Stage plays

In stage plays, you can give the actor instructions about how to speak and what to do. They are called *stage directions*.

(MIKE approaches the table where the DRIVER is sitting.)

MIKE: (Anxiously.) Excuse me...
DRIVER: (Bored.) Yeah?

TV and film

For TV and film plays you can also explain what the camera 'sees'.

(A crowded transport cafe. We see MIKE approach the table where the DRIVER is sitting.)

MIKE: (Anxiously.) Excuse me...
DRIVER: (Bored.) Yeah?

(Close-up of MIKE's face.)

Exercises

A **These are two short extracts from a longer conversation:**

Here it is.
Good. I'm glad you managed to get it.
Do you like it?
Let's have a look then . . . well . . .
You don't like it, do you?
Oh no, I wouldn't say that.
I knew you wouldn't like it.

Oh yes. That was a wonderful time.
Yes it was, wasn't it.
Last June it was.
April.
June. Just before my birthday.
It was April. Straight after Easter.
Rubbish.

Decide who is talking to whom. Decide *how* they say what they say.
Write each conversation as a script with instructions about how the
lines are to be spoken.

B **These are two further extracts from conversations:**

Helena!
Yes?
Can you hear me?
Only just.
I can't speak any louder.

Who's there?
Wouldn't you like to know.
Who is it?
Why don't you come and find out?

Choose one of the extracts and write it out twice:
a as a radio script
b as a stage script

C **Choose one of the extracts from Exercise B and write the whole
conversation from which it comes. Write it as a radio script, or a stage
script.**

Direct speech

Direct speech is the way in which conversations are written down in stories.

1 The words spoken are always put in inverted commas:
    single '_____'
    or double "_____"

2 Each new piece of speech begins with a capital letter.

3 Each piece of speech ends with one of these:

    ,   .   ?   !

4 If you put the *he said* words before the speech, put a comma before the inverted commas:
    He said, '_____.'

5 If you put the *he said* words in the middle of a piece of speech, follow them with a comma or a full stop:
    '_____,' he said, '_____.'
    or '_____,' he said. '_____.'

6 If you follow the *he said* words with a full stop, the next piece of speech must begin with a capital letter.
    'That'll do,' said Mike. 'That'll do fine.'

7 Otherwise a capital letter is not needed:
    'I'm sorry,' he said, 'but I've got to go.'

8 Every time there is a new speaker, start a new line, and indent.

Mike went into the transport cafe. It was very crowded. He saw a lorry driver sitting alone in one corner and made his way across to him. He felt very nervous.
    'Excuse me,' he began.
    'Yeah?' said the driver in a bored voice.
    'Could you give me a lift?'
    'Where to?' asked the driver.
    'How far are you going?'
    'Warrington.'
    'That'll do,' said Mike. 'That'll do fine.'

A   **Here is a short piece of conversation:**

> Hey you!
> Yes? What do you want?
> Come here.
> What for?

In direct speech we have to make it clear who says what:

> 'Hey you!' shouted the policeman.
> 'Yes?' answered the man. 'What do you want?'
> 'Come here,' ordered the policeman.
> 'What for?' asked the man.

Choose one of the extracts that follows. Decide who the people are and who says what. Write the extract as direct speech.

> Got the matches?
> Yes.
> Well come on then.
> Wait a minute.
> You've forgotten them, haven't you?
> No. Here they are.
> Right. Now then . . .
> Watch out. You'll have the whole place on fire!

> Now then, we've got you, haven't we?
> Leave off.
> Why should I?
> I'll get my brother on you.
> Your brother?
> Yes.
> Big deal.

> Aren't you ready yet?
> No I've just got to . . .
> If you don't get a move on, we'll be late.
> Yes but . . .
> But what?
> Well, do we have to go?

B   **Choose a second extract. Think about it carefully and decide how the whole conversation begins and ends. Now write the whole conversation in direct speech.**

C   **How many different words can you think of to use instead of *said*? Make a list of as many as you can think of.**

D   **Rewrite the conversation you did for B, without using the word *said* at all.**

Using a dictionary

cy-cle (′saɪk°l) *n.* **1.** a recurring period of time in which certain events or phenomena occur and reach completion or repeat themselves in a regular sequence. **2.** a completed series of events that follows or is followed by another series of similar events occurring in the same sequence. **3.** the time taken or needed for one such series. **4.** a vast period of time: age, aeon. **5.** a group of poems or prose narratives forming a continuous story about a central figure or event: *the Arthurian cycle.* **6.** a series of miracle plays: *the Chester cycle.* **7.** a group or sequence of songs (see **song-cycle**). **8.** short for **bicycle, tricycle, motorcycle, etc. 9.** *Astronomy,* the orbit of a celestial body. **10.** a recurrent series of events or processes in plants and animals: *a life cycle; a growth cycle.* **11.** *Physics.* a continuous change or a sequence of changes in the state of a system that leads to the restoration of the system to its original state after a finite period of time. **12.** one of a series of repeated changes in the magnitude of a periodically varying quantity such as current or voltage. **13.** *Computer technol.* **a.** a set of operations that can be both treated and repeated as a unit. **b.** the time required to complete a set of operations. **14.** (in generative grammar) the set of cyclic rules. ~*vb.* **15.** (*tr.*) to process through a cycle or system. **16.** (*intr.*) to move in or pass through cycles. **17.** to travel by or ride a bicycle or tricycle.   [C14: from Late Latin *cyclus,* from Greek *kuklos* cycle, circle, ring, wheel; see WHEEL]

Collins English Dictionary

The dictionary provides many different kinds of information about a word.

1 Pronunciation

This special spelling of the word explains how it is pronounced. There is usually an explanation of how it works at the beginning of the dictionary.

2 Part(s) of speech

These abbreviations tell you what part of speech a word is.

n. or sub.	= noun
a. or adj.	= adjective
v. or vb.	= verb
adv.	= adverb

3 Definition(s)

If there are several different meanings, these are numbered.

4 Compounds

How the word can be built up into other words.

5 Phrases

Common phrases in which the word is used.

6 Etymology

Where the word came from.

Exercises

A **Use a dictionary to help you find the correct word to fill the space in each of these sentences.**

1 My brother has just got a provisional driving .... (licence/license).
2 The experiment was done according to strict scientific .... (principals/principles).
3 I found his story quite .... (incredible/incredulous).
4 A horoscope .... (prophecies/prophesies) what will happen to people.
5 If you are going to be good at a sport you need to .... (practice/practise).
6 The strange man wearing a green cloak is going into that old house to .... (exercise/exorcise) a ghost.

B **Each of the words in bold type has more than one meaning. For each sentence, write down the correct dictionary definition of that word.**

1 He needs three more people to **staff** his shop.
2 There are 35 bars **rest** in the middle of that piece of music.
3 He found it difficult to **express** what he was feeling.
4 Don't say a word: keep **mum**.
5 He was wearing a pair of **mules**.
6 He told the barber to **crop** his son's hair.
7 The field was full of **hops**.
8 All his father did was **rail** at him.
9 He thought it was a **novel** idea to work all night and sleep all day.
10 Your **late** aunt was very fond of strawberries.

C **Find out the meaning of each of the words in bold type.**

1 **Radiation** can cause **genetic mutations**.
2 His **bankruptcy** reduced the family to **penury**.
3 He **propounded** the **theory** that school was too much fun these days.
4 No one was listening so his **address** was a **soliloquy**.
5 Hilary was very **haughty**: she **disdained** to talk to the rest of us.

D **Make up your own dictionary definitions for each of these words:**

disco
computer
vandalism
unisex
shuttle

Parts of a word

Words can be made up of three parts:

PREFIX	+	STEM	+	SUFFIX
un		forget		able

Words can therefore be divided into four groups:

1 stem only   appoint
2 prefix + stem   disappoint
3 stem + suffix   appointment
4 prefix + stem + suffix   disappointment

Common prefixes

aero–	ambi–	anti–	audio–	centi–
com–	con–	de–	di–	dis–
electro–	ex–	extra–	il–	im–
in–	inter–	intro–	micro–	milli–
mini–	mis–	mono–	multi–	non–
of–	off–	op–	out–	over–
per–	photo–	post–	pre–	pro–
radio–	re–	semi–	stereo–	sub–
suc–	suf–	sum–	super–	sur–
tele–	trans–	un–	uni–	well–

Common suffixes

–ability	–able	–acy	–al	–ance
–ancy	–ant	–ary	–ate	–ation
–ative	–bility	–ble	–cy	–en
–ence	–er	–ery	–faction	–fic
–ful	–fy	–gram	–graph	–graphy
–ibility	–ible	–ic	–ical	–ician
–icity	–ion	–ious	–ise	–ish
–ism	–ist	–ition	–itious	–ive
–ize	–less	–like	–logy	–ly
–ment	–ness	–or	–ory	–ous
–ry	–sion	–some	–tion	–ty

Exercises

A   **Divide these words up into their separate parts.**

cleverness   unacceptable   radiophonic
accessible   superstitious   telephone
geography   satisfaction   minimise
astrology   politician   history

B   **Add prefixes to these stems to make new words.**

allow   plane   sonic
wisher   graph   cede
approve   happy   grade
circle   head   metre

C   **Add suffixes to these stems to make new words.**

account   fight   aim
light   bribe   hope
quick   excite   debt

D   **Each of these groups of words has one part in common. Study the words and work out what that part means.**

*multi*fold   *astro*naut   *tele*phone
*multi*ply   *astro*nomy   *tele*gram
*multi*ple   *astro*logy   *tele*vision
*multi*tude

graph   bio*logy*
tele*graph*   geo*logy*
*graph*ology
*graph*ic

Syllables

Words can be divided into syllables. You can count the number of syllables in a word by saying it aloud and counting the number of 'beats' it has.

1 syllable : cat   bow   fought   twinge
2 syllables: deny   happy   draughty
3 syllables: superman   excitement   telephoned
4 syllables: radiation   American   complicated
5 syllables: examination   unexcitedly

Haiku A haiku is a short poem with three lines. It has a total of seventeen syllables arranged in a special way.

1st line   : 5 syllables
2nd line   : 7 syllables
3rd line   : 5 syllables

Here is an example:

In	mo	ments	of	joy		
1	2	3	4	5		
all	of	us	wished	we	po	ssessed
1	2	3	4	5	6	7
a	tail	we	could	wag		
1	2	3	4	5		

W. H. Auden

Other examples

With your fists ablaze
with letters and coloured stamps
beautiful mailman

Paul Goodman

Orange and golden
the *New York Times* is blazing
in the village dump

Paul Goodman

A **Write down the number of syllables in each of these words.**

window   carpet   bicycle   shoe   write   comic   coffee
car   bottle   greenhouse

B **Write down the number of syllables in each of these words.**

confess   December   embarrassed   telephone   disapproval
excitement   revolution   factory   chrysanthemum
screwdriver

C **Write down the number of syllables in each of these phrases and clauses.**

in the late summer
a man walking through the fields
happiness and sadness
the machines stopped turning
ship disappearing across the sea

D **Which of these phrases and clauses has the right number of syllables to be the first line of a haiku?**

Two fading roses
Footprints in the frozen snow
A rusting bicycle
Like golden eagles
Grandfather's tired feet
The city streets are silent
A dead bird, frozen
Icicles like spears
Golden rustling leaves
Summer has left us

Spelling: rules

1   Long and short vowels

Long: t*a*pe   rec*e*de   gl*i*de   h*o*pe   f*u*me
Short: t*a*p   b*e*g   gr*i*t   h*o*p   sh*u*t

Adding –ing and –ed: tape   taping   taped
                        tap   tapping   tapped

2   ie/ei

Rule: 'i before e except after c when the sound is long ee'.

ie: field   believe
ei: receive   conceited

Exceptions: seize   weird

3   -ly

We add –ly to adjectives to make them into adverbs.

a   With most words, just add –ly: sad   sadly
b   For words that end in –l still add –ly: hopeful   hopefully
c   For words that end in –ll add –y: dull   dully
d   For words that end in –y, change the –y to –i and then add –ly:
      happy   happily

4   Words that end in -y

a   If you add –s to a word that ends in –y, the spelling usually
      changes. The –y changes to –ie-:   cry   cries
b   If it is a verb that you make past by adding –ed a similar thing
      happens: cry   cried
c   If you add –ing, you do not change the –y: cry   crying
d   If the letter before the –y is a vowel, it does not change to an –i-:
      play   plays   played
e   There are three exceptions to **d**:
      lay becomes laid;   pay becomes paid;   say becomes said.

5   Plurals

Plural means more than one. Most words follow these rules.

a   Normally just add –s: table   tables
b   With words that end –s, add –es: boss   bosses
c   With words that end –ch, add –es: crunch   crunches
d   With words that end –f, change the –f to –ve: half   halves
e   With words that end in –y see rule 4 above.

6   -er,   -ar   -or

To make certain verbs into nouns we add –r or –er.

make   maker
design   designer

There are other words that end with the same sound as –er, but are spelled differently. These just have to be learned. The commonest are as follows:

-ar		**-or**
beggar	particular	actor
burglar	peculiar	doctor
calendar	pillar	inspector
circular	popular	sailor
familiar	regular	visitor
liar	vinegar	

7   -ful   -fully

If we add –full to a word, it becomes –ful. If we then add –ly, it becomes –fully.

shame + full = shameful
shameful + ly = shamefully

8   Words easily confused

here/hear	new/knew	now/know/no
loose/lose	choose/chose	there/their/they're
to/two/too	weather/whether	where/were
who's/whose	right/write	your/you're

9   Single and double letters

accelerate	fulfil	sheriff
accommodation	happiness	success
address	illustrate	sufficient
assist	imitate	terrible
beginning	immediate	transmit
brilliant	marvel	unnecessary
caterpillar	mattress	woollen
collapse	necessary	
collect	occasion	
commit	emission	
corridor	paraffin	
disappear	patrol	
discuss	pedal	
embarrass	possess	
exaggerate	professional	

Acknowledgements

The publishers would like to thank the following for permission to reproduce photographs:

A. Anholt-White, pp. 21, 107; Ashmolean Museum, Oxford, p. 139; Barnaby's Picture Library, pp. 78, 107; BBC Hulton Picture Library, pp. 78, 124, 150, 154; Camera Press, pp. 1, 31, 78; J. Allan Cash, pp. 13, 99; Cinema Bookshop, pp. 84, 88; Cooper Bridgeman Library, p. 81; Department of the Environment, p. 21; Mary Evans Picture Library, pp. 88, 108, 109; Greater London Council, p. 148; Richard and Sally Greenhill, pp. 121, 153; Illustrated London News, pp. 18, 19; Japanese Tourist Office, p. 78; Keystone Press Agency, pp. 13, 133; Frank W. Lane, p. 44; Mansell Collection, pp. 78, 110, 150; Massey-Ferguson, p. 107; Novosti Press Agency, p. 116; OEC Orthopaedic, p. 107; P & O Cruises Ltd., pp. 95, 96, 97; Popperfoto, pp. 13, 78, 121, 133; TI Raleigh Ltd., pp. 110, 119; Space Frontiers Ltd., p. 74; Syndication International, p. 136; John Topham, pp. 31, 62, 107, 121, 133; Peter G. Wickman/Stern, p. 114.

Illustrations by: Noel Connor, Tony Morris, Peter North, Tony Roberts, Malcolm Stokes, Barrie Thorpe.

Cover photograph courtesy of Camera Press

The publishers would like to thank the following for permission to reprint copyright material:

E. Allen: from *Wartime Children 1939–45* (A. & C. Black, 1975). *Annual Abstract of Statistics 1980*, 'Road Accident Figures for 1977', are reprinted by permission of Her Majesty's Stationery Office. Isaac Asimov: from *I, Robot* (Dobson). W. H. Auden: 'In moments of joy' from *Collected Poems*. Reprinted by permission of Faber & Faber Ltd. Patricia Baker: from *Martin Luther King* (1974). Reprinted by permission of Wayland Publ. Ltd. Richard Ballantine: text and illustrations from *Richard's Bicycle Book* © Richard Ballantine. Reprinted by permission of Pan Books Ltd. Stan Barstow: from *Joby* (1964). Reprinted by permission of Michael Joseph Ltd. Nina Bawden: from *Carrie's War* (1973). Reprinted by permission of Victor Gollancz Ltd. Rachel Billington: from *Sammy's Diary*, from the collection *Dandelion Clocks* ed. Bradley/Jamieson. Reprinted by permission of Michael Joseph Ltd. Betsy Byars: from *The TV Kid* (1976). Reprinted by permission of The Bodley Head. Charles Causley: 'On Being Asked' from *Collected Poems* (Macmillan). Reprinted by permission of David Higham Associates Ltd. Aidan Chambers: from *Funny Folk* (1976). Reprinted by permission of William Heinemann Ltd. Michael Chinery: extract adapted from *The Family Naturalist*. Reprinted by permission of Macdonald Futura Publ. John Christopher: from *The Guardians* (Hamish Hamilton 1970/Puffin 1973). Reprinted by permission of the author. Arthur C. Clarke: extracts from 'An Ape About the House' and 'More About Dorcas' from *Of Time and Stars* (Gollancz). Reprinted by permission of David Higham Associates Ltd. *Collins Dictionary*; extract reprinted by permission of William Collins Sons & Co. Ltd. Roald Dahl: 'The Wish' from *Someone Like You* (Michael Joseph Ltd./Penguin). Reprinted by permission of Murray Pollinger. *Daily Mirror*: extracts reprinted by permission of Syndication International for Mirror Group Newspapers. Peter Freuchen: 'The Mother's Song' from *Peter Freuchen's Book of the Eskimos*, publ. by Arthur Barker Ltd., 1962. Reprinted by permission of George Weidenfeld & Nicolson Ltd. Roy Fuller: 'The National Union of Children' and 'The National Association of Parents' both from *Poor Roy*. Reprinted by permission of Andre Deutsch. Paul Goodman: 'With your fists ablaze' and 'Orange and Golden'. Copyright © 1967 by Paul Goodman. Reprinted from *Collected Poems*, edited by Taylor Stoehr, by permission of Random House Inc. Graham Greene: extract from *The Third Man*, from *The Third Man and Loser Takes All* (Heinemann & The Bodley Head). Reprinted by permission of Laurence Pollinger Ltd. Bryn Griffiths: 'Bleep'. Reprinted by permission of the author. Arthur Grimble: from *A Pattern of Islands* (1952). Reprinted by permission of John Murray (Publ.) Ltd. Seamus Heaney: 'Blackberry Picking' from *Death of a Naturalist*. Reprinted by permission of Faber & Faber Ltd. Susan Hill: from

I'm the King of the Castle (1970). Reprinted by permission of Hamish Hamilton Ltd. Langston Hughes: 'Aunt Sue's Stories'. Copyright 1926 by Alfred A. Knopf, Inc., and renewed 1954 by Langston Hughes. Reprinted from *Selected Poems of Langston Hughes* by permission of Alfred A. Knopf, Inc. Ted Hughes: 'The Warrior in Winter' from *Season Songs*. Reprinted by permission of Faber & Faber Ltd. Laurie Lee: from *Cider With Rosie* (1959). Reprinted by permission of the author and The Hogarth Press Ltd. C. S. Lewis: from *Perelandra* (1943). Reprinted by permission of The Bodley Head. Edward Lowbury: 'Prince Kano' from *Green Magic* (Chatto). Reprinted by permission of the author. David Macaulay: from *Underground* © David Macaulay 1976. Reprinted by permission of Collins Publ. George MacBeth: 'Bedtime Story' from *The Broken Places* (Scorpion Press). Reprinted by permission of the author. Norman MacCaig: 'Brooklyn Cop' from *Selected Poems*. Reprinted by permission of the author and The Hogarth Press Ltd. Lewis Mackenzie: 'Three Haiku' by Kobayashi Issa, translated by Lewis Mackenzie, from *The Autumn Wind*. Reprinted by permission of John Murray (Publ.) Ltd. Edwin Morgan: 'The First Men on Mercury' from *From Glasgow to Saturn* (1973). Reprinted by permission of Carcanet Press. Farley Mowat: from *Never Cry Wolf*. Reprinted by permission of Hughes Massie Ltd., for the author and Pan Books Ltd. Errol O'Connor: from *Jamaica Child*, in *Our Lives* (ILEA English Centre, 1979). Reprinted by permission. Gareth Owen: 'Cycling Down the Street to Meet My Friend John' from *Salford Road* (Kestrel Books, 1979) p. 13. Copyright © 1971, 1974, 1976, 1979 by Gareth Owen. Reprinted by permission of Penguin Books Ltd. George D. Painter: 'When George began to climb . . .' was first published in *The Road to Sinodun* by G. D. Painter (Hart-Davis, 1951) and is reprinted by permission of the author. Tony Parker: from *The Unknown Citizen* (Hutchinson). James Reeves: from *Islands and Palaces* (1971). Reprinted by permission of Blackie & Son Ltd. Glasgow. Patrick Rivers: from *The Restless Generation* (Davis-Poynter). Reprinted by permission of the author. Carl Sandburg: 'Get off this Estate' from *The People, Yes*, copyright 1936 by Harcourt Brace Jovanovich, Inc.; copyright 1964 by Carl Sandburg. Reprinted by permission of the publisher. Clancy Sigal: from *Weekend In Dinlock* (1960). Reprinted by permission of Martin Secker & Warburg Ltd. Lil Smith: from *The Good Old Bad Old Days* (1975). Reprinted by permission of the author and Centreprise. Tom Stoppard (page 15): from *Rosencrantz and Guildenstern are Dead*. Reprinted by permission of Faber & Faber Ltd. May Swenson: 'Southbound on the Freeway' from *New & Selected Things Taking Place* © 1963 by May Swenson. First appeared in *The New Yorker*. Reprinted by permission of Little, Brown & Company. Paul Theroux: from *The Great Railway Bazaar* (Hamish Hamilton). Reprinted by permission of Gillon Aitken. Dylan Thomas: from *Quite Early One Morning* (Dent). Reprinted by permission of David Higham Associates Ltd. Leslie Thomas: from *This Time Next Week* (1967). Reprinted by permission of Constable Publ. Flora Thompson: from *Lark Rise to Candleford* (1954). Reprinted by permission of Oxford University Press. H. G. Wells: from *The War of the Worlds*. Reprinted by permission of A. P. Watt Ltd. for the Estate of H. G. Wells and William Heinemann. Laura Ingalls Wilder: from *The Long Winter*. Reprinted by permission of Lutterworth Press. Eric Williams: from *The Tunnel* by Eric Williams, published in the UK by Wm. Collins Sons & Co. Ltd. Reprinted by permission of the author.
Ogden Nash: 'The Canary', 'The Shark' and 'The Bat' from *Collected Poems*. Reprinted by permission of Curtis Brown Ltd., London, on behalf of the Estate of Ogden Nash.
D'Arcy Niland: from *Dadda Jumped Over Two Elephants*. Reprinted by permission of Curtis Brown Ltd., on behalf of the Estate of D'Arcy Niland.

Every effort has been made to trace and contact copyright holders but this has not always been possible. We apologise for any infringement of copyright.